Arctic Routes to Fabled Lands

Arctic Routes to Fabled Lands

*Olivier Brunel and the Passage to China and Cathay
in the Sixteenth Century*

Marijke Spies

Translated from Dutch by Myra Heerspink Scholz

AMSTERDAM UNIVERSITY PRESS

The author and publisher gratefully acknowledge the assistance of the Prins Bernhard Fonds.

Original title: *Bij Noorden om*
Cover illustration: Gerard Mercator, *The North Pole Area*, from the 1595 *Atlas, pars altera*, map. no. 1. Photo © Maritiem Museum 'Prins Hendrik', Rotterdam
Cover design: Kok Korpershoek [ko], Amsterdam
Typesetting: MAGENTA, Amsterdam

ISBN 90 5356 263 x

But it were to be wished, that non would write Histories with so great a desire of setting foorth novelties and strange things, [...][1]

Arngrimus Ionas Islandus 1592

---

1   Hakluyt 1 1598, p.561.

Contents

I   *The Man*

His name crops up out of nowhere, vanishes, then appears again. The four or five times he is mentioned in documents, some of them separated by decades, suggest a life lived as one long journey through the countries of northern Europe. From trading settlement to commercial center, from harbor town back to trading settlement—a handful of cabins at the mouth of a river, hamlets with names long since forgotten.

This much we know: sometime in the middle of the sixteenth century Olivier Brunel, native of Brussels or Louvain, was sent from Kola on the north coast of Lapland to Kholmogory, situated on the lower reaches of the river Dvina, for the purpose of learning Russian.[1] Sent by whom?

Few ships ventured around North Cape at this time (see ill. 1). The oldest Dutch maritime map, from 1543, extended only a little beyond Bergen on the Norwegian coast, and the earliest sailing instructions, dated 1551, went as far as Trondheim.[2] And why should anyone have wanted to sail farther? Most of the trade with Russia followed the Baltic routes, via the Hanse cities Narva, Riga, Reval and Novgorod, where the Dutch had a trading post of their own.

For more than two centuries the league of Hanse towns had guarded its monopoly by obstructing any direct contact between western Europe and Russia. But in the

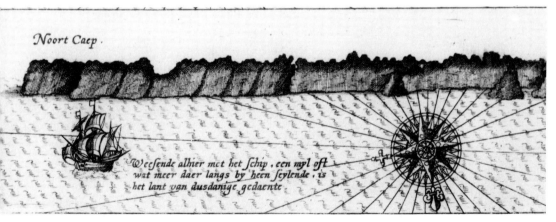

1.   Jan Huyghen van Linschoten, *North Cape*.

1   Jansma 1946, p. 343-344; Horensma 1985, p. 124.
2   Burger 1915, p. 211; Schilder 1984, p. 493.

2. Lucas Janszoon Waghenaer, *Europe* (1583).
   Extent of Dutch seafaring in nordic areas before 1565.

course of the sixteenth century this commercial bulwark began to face challenges from both sides. The Russian Tsar Ivan IV, known as Ivan the Terrible (or, more accurately perhaps, the Awesome), directed his attention to the west, in matters both military and commercial. At the same time merchants from England and newly flourishing trading centers in the Low Countries, such as Antwerp and Enkhuizen, were searching for alternative routes in order to escape the clutches of the Hanse. They intensified their efforts as the tsar's conflicts with Poland and Sweden rendered the Baltic less safe.

A route around the top of Norway was a possibility. There, between North Cape and the White Sea lay Vardöhus, a fortified Danish toll station; and a short distance beyond, on a fjord below the peninsula Kegor, was a Russian monastery (see ill. 2). A little farther yet lay Kola, also Russian, a hamlet of only three or four houses where the monks came to trade textiles and beer for whale oil, stockfish and hides. In 1557 Stephen Burrough, commissioned by the English Company of Merchant Adventurers for the Discovery of Lands, Territories, Isles, Dominions and Seignories Unknown, reported that he had encountered Dutch merchants in Kola.[3] In any case we know for sure that eight years later a certain Philip Winterkoning from Ooltgensplaat, together with six associates from Antwerp, Bruges and Enkhuizen, was conducting trade with Russians from the Lapp Muncke (Monks') Fjord.[4]

The English had already penetrated farther, and were now at the mouth of the Dvina on the White Sea. They had begun exploring the northern route for entirely different reasons. What they hoped to find was a north-east passage to China and the mysterious, fabulously rich land of Cathay, thought to lie to the north of, and partly overlapping with, China. Already in 1553 a first expedition of three ships set out under the command of Hugh Willoughby, Stephen Burrough and Richard Chancellor. The two ships of Willoughby ran aground off the coast of Lapland. There they would be found two years later in the muddy waters of the Arzina River, with the bodies of the seventy crew members who had frozen to death. But the third ship with Burrough and Chancellor sailed on and eventually reached the White Sea. From there Chancellor traveled overland to Moscow.

This opened the door for direct trade with Russia. For the next few decades the English company devoted more of its attention to commerce with the Russians than to the uncertainties of a northeast passage. Burrough did make a voyage that went beyond Novaya Zemlya in 1556, but on his way back he founded a trading settlement on a Danish island in the Dvina, opposite the St. Nicholas monastery, and this became the focus of English activity for the time being.[5] About sixty kilometers farther upriver was Brunel's destination, Kholmogory.

It is tempting to look for a connection between this first mention of Olivier Brunel and the business ventures of Philip Winterkoning and associates. They had been granted the charter for sea trade with the "Northland" as far as Moscow by the sovereign of the Seventeen Dutch Provinces, Philip II, and his regent, Margaret of Parma. Along with the charter came letters of recommendation to all monarchs and potentates in the

---

3   Ahvenainen 1967, p. 13-14; Starkov 1993, p. 21.
4   Jansma 1946, p. 338-343.
5   Linschoten 1914, p. xxxv-xxxvi; Willan 1968, p. 3-6 and 15.

region, requesting them to assist the company by providing ships, wagons, horses and drivers, all against fair payment. Winterkoning left Kola in a rented Russian vessel in 1565 and set course for St. Nicholas with the intention of traveling on from there to Moscow. But he did not get far. Just off the coast of Lapland his ship was attacked by the crew of another Russian ship. It was a harsh world. The thirteen Russians accompanying Winterkoning had their throats cut in their sleep. Although wounded himself, Winterkoning managed to reach land, but was then felled by an arrow shot from behind a tree. His business partners, Simon van Salingen and Cornelius de Meyer, were not about to take this lying down. Later that same year De Meyer set out for Moscow to lodge an official complaint. Already in Novgorod, however, he was detained and told that the Grand Duke would be offended because he had not been addressed with the proper titles in the charter letter; moreover a complaint would not even reach him because the commander in Novgorod had been bribed by both the murderers and the English; and furthermore, the English did not want anyone interfering with their trade via St. Nicholas. All this lends credence to the idea of some collusion on the part of the English in the murderous raid. A monopoly was literally worth a fortune, and an emissary from a competing trading company represented a very real threat.

Upon returning to Kola, De Meyer and Van Salingen planned their next line of attack for the following year. Disguised as Russians and with a retinue of Russian servants, they set out for Moscow once again. This time they did reach the capital. There they got in touch with a former business acquaintance, who was unable to help them,

3.   *Kola on the North Coast of Lapland.*
     A small cluster of houses with Russian merchants and native Lapps.

however, because their secret travel route, their Russian clothing, and their lack of offi-cial travel documents now made them appear as spies.[6] At this same time the represen-tative of the English Muscovy Company, Anthony Jenkinson, was in Moscow, attempting to secure from the tsar the monopoly on White Sea trade for his company. In September of 1567 he succeeded.[7]

In Kholmogory, sometime during these same years, the English convinced the Rus-sians that Olivier Brunel was a spy. He was first taken to Moscow, then two hundred miles farther north, to the town of Yaroslavl', where he was held prisoner for several years. Unlikely as it seems, this proved to be a stroke of luck, for there he was eventual-ly discovered by the most enterprising of all families in the world of Russian commerce and industry, the Stroganovs.[8]

In the meantime Dutch trade with Kola was steadily expanding. Winterkoning's partnership fell apart after his death, but his associates continued the trade, both indi-vidually and together with new partners. In 1567, again in 1569, 1570 and the years fol-lowing, ships arrived from Enkhuizen and Bergen op Zoom, then from a large number of other Netherlandic ports. They steered a course close to shore around North Cape, past Vardöhus and the peninsula Ribachi (then called Kegor), for no one knew what lay farther north. From the Russian side, too, increasing numbers of "lodyas," small ships with one transverse sail, were setting course for Lapland. The Lapps brought their hides, salmon and whale oil, only to disappear again into the vast landscape as quickly as they had come, a strange, shy people whose language no one could understand. They conducted their trade with gestures, and were gone, gliding off in their reindeer sleighs or skimming like phantoms over the snow on wooden slats attached to their feet (see ill. 19 and 20). But the Russians stayed. Already in 1572 the settlement, presumably some-where near present-day Murmansk, numbered about two hundred people, not includ-ing the fifty monks from the monastery.[9] Kola was now a cluster of buildings on the steep, rocky coast: a stockade with watch-towers on the four corners, a gallows, a chapel, and between the houses fish drying on poles above smoldering fires (see ill. 3).

A little less than eight hundred kilometers northwest of Moscow lies Sol'vychegodsk, the site of Anika Stroganov's salt works. The salt went to Moscow, and soon furs, rein-deer hides and fish were sent there as well. Over the years Anika's trade expanded to St. Nicholas and Kola in the north, where he exchanged his hides for products from the west, and to the Urals in the east. Between 1558 and 1568 he and his sons Grigory and Yakov obtained from Ivan the Terrible sovereign rights to the entire region around pre-sent-day Perm in the east. There they mined and smelted iron ore. They also sent expe-ditions across the Urals into Siberia, homeland of the Tartars, in search of sable and ermine, for these most precious furs could be sold for fabulous prices in Moscow and for even more in the west.[10]

---

6   Linschoten 1914, p. xl-xli and Appendix I, p. 211-216.
7   Willan 1968, p. 88-90.
8   Jansma 1946, p. 344; Durme 1959, nr. 143, p. 158-159; Wassenaer 1625, p. 93.
9   Linschoten 1914, Appendix I, p. 219-220.
10   Fischer 1768, p. 181-186; Fisher 1943, p. 24-25.

In all these activities the Stroganovs employed westerners for their expertise. A German physician, for example, had accompanied Anika from Kola to dig precious stones from the river Iksa at the Finnish border, and an Englishman commissioned by the king's ambassador in Moscow instructed them in the building of smelteries in the Urals.[11] They were also on the lookout for foreign prisoners. Olivier Brunel was almost bound to be found by them sooner or later, since travelers from Sol'vychegodsk to Moscow inevitably passed through Yaroslavl', as they still do today. So it was that after a few years of imprisonment Brunel entered the service of the Stroganovs.

He was commissioned to travel down the Volga, from Kazan' all the way south to Astrakhan on the Caspian Sea, the same route repeatedly taken by the Englishman Jenkinson.[12] He also took part in one of their expeditions to Siberia, as far as the Ob', the enormous river that flows from Tomsk in the south to the Arctic Ocean. No one from western Europe, including Jenkinson, had ever gone this far.

According to some reports Brunel managed to reach the mouth of the Ob' by sea, which would mean that he sailed east from St. Nicholas, past Novaya Zemlya, as no one but Burrough had done before, except perhaps the odd Russian in a lightly laden lodya.[13]

In any case, in July of 1576 he returned to Kola, still in the service of the Stroganovs and in the company of two members of their family, with a heavy load of hides and other goods. On August 6th he set sail for the Netherlands and on September 11th was in Dordrecht, an important market town of long standing. Here, but no doubt mainly in Antwerp and Paris, their next destinations, they sold their cargo of elk hides, sable and other merchandise.[14]

For Brunel this must have been an emotional homecoming. At the time of his departure the southern Netherlands was riding a wave of prosperity, with Antwerp its bustling center of commerce and industry. Now there was war. Since 1572, when the Protestant rebels conquered Den Briel, a large part of Holland and Zeeland had broken away from the Spanish king and the central government in Brussels. The two regions had joined forces under the leadership of William, Prince of Orange. Although most of the skirmishes had taken place on the territory of these two provinces, it was precisely in 1576 that the tide turned drastically. The southern provinces were suddenly ravaged by the mutiny of the Spanish troops. Having for years received no payment for their services, they roamed the countryside, plundering as they went. Trading activities, which had already been suffering from years of conflict, stagnated further. But the greatest disaster for Antwerp was still to come. During the first days of November the city fell prey to the Spanish Fury: eight thousand people were murdered, six hundred houses set afire, and booty valued at one and a half million guilders—in today's terms between one and two hundred million guilders—was carried off.[15]

Around this time Brunel must have been in Antwerp, where he made contact with Jan van de Walle of the Gillis Hooftman Company. He might have been renewing an

---

11   Semjonow n.d., p. 37-38 and 51-52.
12   Williamson 1922, p. 114.
13   Jansma 1946, p. 344; Hakluyt 1 1598, p. 511; Linschoten 1914, p. xlii-xliii and p. 229 and 234.
14   Jansma 1946, p. 357-358.
15   Groenveld-Leeuwenberg 1979, p. 96-98; Parker 1981, p. 163-172.

earlier acquaintance, for Hooftman had been active on the market for about twenty years. This might even explain why Brunel was so important to the Stroganovs, for in these times buying and selling was largely a matter of personal relationships. In any case, war or no war, business went on.

In 1577 Brunel and Jan van de Walle traveled to Russia together and set up a new association there for trade via Kola.[16] Merchants from the northern Netherlands must have been involved as well. At least we know that the Danish king, Frederick II, who was also the sovereign of Norway, protested to the municipal government of Amsterdam and the Prince of Orange, as well as to the town councils of Dordrecht and Flushing. Kola, he insisted, fell under his jurisdiction. There might be some Russian squatters but they had no right to be there, and trade could only be conducted by parties who had received his permission and who paid him toll. The latter was, of course, the crux of the matter. But all that his protest achieved was that cargoes were now no longer transferred at Kola but at the mouth of the Dvina on the White Sea. Not at the Danish St. Nicholas, of course, where the English had installed themselves, but on a small island one mile farther east which fell under Russian jurisdiction. There, at the Podesyemsco mouth of the Dvina, Jan van de Walle established himself as an agent for Gillis Hooftman. Six miles upstream, near the St. Michael monastery, a new city would be founded in 1583 by decree of the tsar of all Russians: New Kholmogory, or—as the people soon came to call it —Archangel, after the archangel Michael.[17] There was no need to worry about the English, for their monopoly had been disintegrating ever since 1570, the year Queen Elizabeth I humiliated the tsar by refusing his hand in marriage.[18]

One can imagine that Brunel, remembering how the English had betrayed him in the old Kholmogory, was now laughing up his sleeve. This was the world of commerce. Kings and governments fought for positions of power: Philip II of Spain against the Dutch cities led by the Prince of Orange, Frederick II of Denmark against Holstein and Sweden, and Tsar Ivan IV of Russia against Poland and Sweden. But in the meantime trading companies—the Stroganovs, the Hooftmans—made their contacts. Their agents sailed the seas, and criss-crossed Europe on one postal horse after another. Like ants they dragged their goods over endless distances: a load of wax to be traded for linens or a shipment of wine; salmon and whale oil from Kola, tallow, flax and rope from Russia for salt from Portugal and silk from Italy or the Levant; and especially furs from the north for pepper from the south. Wherever something of value could be found they went to get it. The quantities which agents like Philip Winterkoning and Olivier Brunel purchased and transported through the damp, mud, and cold from one or another desolate corner of the world were never large, but for that very reason they were precious. Profits accumulated and were reinvested, or given as loans to warring governments, or seized by plundering soldiers.

The Stroganovs, however, had even greater aspirations. In 1574 Ivan the Terrible ordered them to start planning the conquest of Siberia. In advance they were given possession of the entire area around the rivers Tura and Tobol. The first attempt was made

16 Fisher 1943, p. 24 and 191; Wijnroks 1993, p. 46.
17 Wassenaer 8 1625, p. 91 recto-verso; Kernkamp 1903, p. 262-263; Jansma 1946, p. 344-345 and 347; Starkov 1993, p. 21-22; Wijnroks 1993, p. 50-51.
18 Laughton 1892, p. 308.

in 1579. Commissioned by Anika's youngest son Semyon and his grandsons Maxim Yakovlevich and Nikita Grigorevich, the Cossack leader Yermak invaded Siberia with only about a thousand soldiers. He managed to put three to four hundred kilometers behind him, and even to occupy the stronghold Sibir, seat of the ruling khan, before being defeated by the Tartars and then drowning in the Irtysh River in 1584.[19]

Was this exploit perhaps part of a larger scheme to explore the rivers of northern Russia for a trade route to Cathay? Interest in this possibility was growing again. In 1580 Arthur Pet and Charles Jackman set out on a new mission for the English Merchant Adventurers—or the Muscovy Company, as the firm had been called for the last several years—following the route taken by Burrough along the coast of Novaya Zemlya, in search of a northeast passage. The instructions to the two leaders of the expedition and Queen Elizabeth's letters to the rulers of lands unknown indicate just how high the expectations were. The assignment was to sail through the passage Burrough had discovered between Novaya Zemlya and Vaygach Island, along the coast of the Kara Sea to the mouth of the Ob', and on from there to Cathay. An important condition was added to these general directives, however: if the coastline beyond the Ob' should appear to make a sharp bend to the north, as far as the eightieth parallel or—as the Flemish cartographer Ortelius assumed—even farther, they would have to spend the winter in the Ob' estuary. The following year they were then to sail as far as possible upriver and attempt to reach the city of Sibir.[20]

When the cartographer Mercator, who lived in Duisburg, heard about the departure of this expedition in July of 1580, he quickly sent a letter to the English geographer Richard Hakluyt in Oxford. He regretted that he had been unable to give advice, and emphatically recommended the second option. In his opinion there were large, easily navigable rivers flowing from one end of the continent to the other, which would form an excellent trade connection with China and Cathay.[21]

At this time Brunel was entertaining similar ideas of his own. He was the only person who had reached the Ob' on an earlier occasion, and he had probably done so both by way of the Kara Sea and by land. He was also the only one who had actually been in Sibir on the Irtysh, tributary of the Ob'. Some time around February of 1581 he paid a visit to the merchant Johan Balakus, who lived in Arensberg on Ösel, a Baltic island near Riga. Brunel told him he was on his way to Antwerp, on a mission for the Stroganovs, to recruit seamen for an expedition to Cathay. In New Kholmogory at the mouth of the Dvina two ships were already being built for this purpose. This voyage, too, would proceed through the Kara Sea to the Ob'. Brunel maintained that a twelve-day journey up the Ob' would bring them to a city called Yaks Olgush, which he had previously reached by an overland route. The people living there had reported seeing richly laden ships sailing on the river Ardoh, three days farther upstream. And the Ardoh, they claimed, flowed into Lake Kittay, which bordered the Kingdom of Cathay.[22]

19   Fischer 1768, p. 186-246; Lengyel 1949, p. 36-39; Fisher 1943, p. 25-27.
20   Hakluyt 1 1598, p. 433-435; cf. Ortelius 1570 (1964) map 47 "Tartaria"; Horensma 1985, p. 125.
21   Hakluyt 1 1598, p. 444-445; Durme 1959, nr. 143, p. 158-159.
22   Hakluyt 1 1598, p. 511-512.

None of this is very clear. The maps which Ortelius and Mercator published around this time show the Ob', the fortified city of Sibir and Lake Kittay, but nothing of a city called Yaks Olgush or, more importantly, the river Ardoh, which was supposed to be the essential link in the east-west connection.[23] Brunel's story does show some similarity to the description of Siberia published in 1549 by Siegmund von Herberstein, an account acquired by this German diplomat during one of his visits to Moscow.[24] But neither Brunel nor Herberstein—nor the cartographers—could have had any idea of the thousands of miles one would have to travel east before reaching the area where Cathay was thought to lie, northeast of India and Cambodia, toward the east coast of the continent. Probably the part of the route familiar to Brunel extended no farther than the sharp eastward bend in the Ob' where it is joined by the Irtysh from the south. Yermak's expedition had set out in precisely this direction. The possibility of an overland route had previously been considered by Anthony Jenkinson, but he had decided against it because of the warlike tribes living there.[25] Perhaps the pacification of the area, and especially the subjugation of the Tartar khan, Kuchum, who ruled Sibir and the region around the Irtysh, was considered a precondition for a successful expedition. Perhaps this was the real motive behind Yermak's campaign.

We know about Brunel's plans from a letter of recommendation dated February 20, 1581 which Johan Balakus addressed to Gerard Mercator in Duisburg. Brunel delivered it to Mercator, who sent it on to Richard Hakluyt together with his own letter about the journey of Pet and Jackman.[26] All over Europe—in Italy, Germany, the southern Netherlands and England—mapmakers and geographers were eagerly incorporating every new shred of information into the world picture they had inherited from the past. Reports from seafarers, travelers and diplomats circulated from one cartographer to another, then back to those for whom geographical knowledge carried promise of profit. Whatever Brunel knew must have had considerable market value.

Brunel himself, however, seems to have been in no hurry to carry out his mission once he was in the Netherlands. Was it perhaps the political and military situation that held him back? Again he arrived in Antwerp at precisely the worst moment. The Spanish Fury had raged during his first homecoming in 1576, and now, in 1581, the abjuration of the Spanish king brought about a definitive split between the southern and northern Netherlands. The effect on trade, however, was mainly limited to a migration of merchants and financiers to northern cities like Middelburg, Enkhuizen and Amsterdam. Another possibility is that Brunel was waiting for news of Jackman. Pet had already returned in 1580 with little to report in the way of success, but nothing further had been heard of Jackman.[27] A more likely reason for Brunel's delay, however, is that he was trying to find investors; for when he finally set out in 1584, the expedition was in large part financed not by the Stroganovs, but by a partnership originating in Antwerp. But this is getting ahead of our story.

---

23   Mercator 1569 (1961), sheet 12; Ortelius 1570 (1964), map 47 "Tartaria."
24   Henning 1906, p. 17-21.
25   Purchas 12 1906, p. 25-26.
26   Hakluyt 1 1598, p. 511-512; Hintzsche 1994, p. 179.
27   Burger 1930, p. 40-45.

While in Antwerp Brunel made contact with Balthasar de Moucheron, the man who would later provide much of the impetus for Netherlandic exploration of northern sea routes, but who at this time was still completely oriented toward Baltic trade via Narva. Brunel and a Norwegian associate from Bergen, Arent Meyer, signed an agreement with the Danish king in the name of Moucheron to undertake at their own cost an exploratory voyage to Greenland. That, of course, meant sailing in the opposite direction from the Kara Sea. And it was an entirely different story.[28]

Greenland had gotten lost. In the thirteenth century the king of Norway had claimed for himself a monopoly on all trade with the two small Viking settlements there. An ombudsman was appointed, and a bishop. But after the Norwegian crown passed into Danish hands in 1380, official contacts were neglected, and in the fifteenth century they broke off completely. All that was left were rumors of a far-off land where the people had turned green from the sea water, and from which mountains of cheese and butter had been imported in times long past. No one knew that the settlers of the western village had already been massacred in the fourteenth century—by Indians or Eskimos perhaps, nothing is known for sure—and that the eastern settlement had gradually died out as a result of inbreeding and malnutrition. But with the rise of long-distance trade the Danish kings came to regret the loss of their western outpost. Already in the 1470's, and again in 1521, 1564 and 1578, ships were dispatched to restore the contact. In vain. No one had a clear idea anymore of the direction or the distance.[29]

Whether Brunel and Meyer actually undertook this expedition is uncertain, although it is not unlikely. In any case Brunel made one or more trips to Denmark, and perhaps to more distant destinations, during those years spent in Antwerp.[30] Only in 1584 did he finally set sail in the direction of the Ob', "situated within the borders of Tartary," with a ship full of merchandise valued at eight thousand florins—in today's reckoning about one and a half million guilders. His associate Meyer had invested one-sixteenth of this amount. The rest came from the Antwerp partnership, probably with the backing of De Moucheron, who was, no doubt, as susceptible as anyone else to the spell of mysterious Cathay.

They left from Enkhuizen, where Brunel had been living for the last year, and where his wife Susanna stayed to await his return. She probably waved good-bye from the pier or from the Dromedary Tower, her eyes straining to see the invisible as the ship grew steadily smaller, her lips forming a last "bon voyage." But the voyage turned out to be anything but good. Nothing came of the original plan to explore the rivers for a route to Cathay, or even of the intention to sail at least as far as the Ob'. Probably the narrow passages to the Kara Sea along Novaya Zemlya were blocked by ice floes. One of the reports which circulated later suggests that this might have been the main obstacle. In any case, Brunel anchored at Novaya Zemlya and, upon finding no one there, sailed back to one of the estuaries on the Russian coast. There he hoped to trade his cargo with the local inhabitants for hides and rock crystal, a highly prized stone at the time. There were handsome profits to be made.

---

28   Jansma 1946, p. 348-350.
29   Lucas 1937, p. 177-178; Hennig 2 1950, p. 283-284 and 3 1953, p. 439-454; Vaughan 1982, p. 334-335.
30   Jansma 1946, p. 349-350.

But what about his commission from the Stroganovs? And the two ships which had been built in New Kholmogory? It looks very much as if Brunel had been trying to avoid Russian merchants. He might even have been quite happy to sail no farther than he did. Before any merchandise actually changed hands, however, the boat he was using to ferry his cargo sank mid-river. Like so many others before and after him, Brunel died in the ice and mud of half-submerged sandbanks in a fog-shrouded corner of the world. Not a Lapp or a Samoyed witnessed it. Or if they saw it, they simply let him drown, then made off with his mirrors and beads and whatever else he had with him.

In any event, the merchandise disappeared. The ship and the rest of the crew returned to Enkhuizen. They brought with them samples of white, blue, and gray rock crystal, but these plus the sale of the ship itself did not yield enough to pay the crew's wages, which meant that the shipowners themselves had to make up the difference.[31]

Despite all this, the idea lived on. Eight years later, in 1593, Balthasar de Moucheron launched his plan to search for a passage to the Indies "by a northern route." A great deal had happened in the meantime: the assassination of William of Orange, his succession by the seventeen-year old Maurice, and the conquest of Antwerp for the Spanish king by the Duke of Parma. De Moucheron had moved to Middelburg and, in 1587, had transferred his trading activities from the Baltic to the mouth of the Dvina on the White Sea.

It was during these same years that the war with Spain led to the growing conviction among merchants and government officials that they would have to find a sea route to the far east themselves. This would render them independent of Portugal, Spain's ally, for imports. It would also be a way of striking a deadly economic blow at their enemy. And, most importantly, they would themselves reap all those wonderful profits.

De Moucheron was able to interest the provincial governments of both Zeeland and Holland, as well as Prince Maurice himself—who was always fascinated by new inventions and discoveries—in his alternative route to the Indies. The name Brunel also started cropping up again, in the writings of De Moucheron, but especially in the famous "mapbook" of Lucas Janszoon Waghenaer, himself a resident of Enkhuizen, the city from which Brunel had set out on his last, fateful journey.[32] This explains how Willem Barents, when anchoring at Novaya Zemlya during his first voyage to the Arctic Ocean in 1594, thought he recognized the spot "where Olivier Brunel had been before."[33]

That was the man and, as far as we know from the clues he left behind, those were his deeds. They formed the prelude to Dutch exploration of the north, which would culminate one decade later in Barents and Heemskerck's spectacular wintering on Novaya Zemlya. But what was that northern world like at the time? What did it mean for a young man from Louvain or Brussels to sail beyond North Cape? And what did the most authoritative scholars of the day say they would find on the other side of the Urals?

---

31   Waghenaer 1592 p. 104; Jansma 1946, p. 350-353.
32   Stoppelaar 1901, p. 94-102; Waghenaer 1592, p. 101, 104 and 204; Linschoten 1914, p. 234.
33   Veer 1 1917, p. 20.

Uncharted territory stretched out on all sides. To the north, through mist and ice, lay the pole. According to some authorities, this was where the streams flowing through the oceans were sucked into the center of the earth; but according to others, the earthly paradise could be found there, tucked among sheltering mountains. To the east lay dark Siberia, home of the Tartars and other tribes, one stranger than the other: Amazons, Cynocephali or dog-headed people, the happy Hyperboreans, Neuri who could change themselves into wolves, and the man-eating Anthropophagi—and beyond all that the legendary Kingdom of Cathay. Uncharted, too, were the expanses along the north coast of Russia, home of the shy Lapps, with their magic and their way of appearing quick as lightning, then vanishing again, and the even shyer Eskimos—Skraelings, Pygmies, they were known by various names. And toward the west, near the volcano Hekla on Iceland, you could hear the souls in Purgatory moaning; and somewhere beyond or above that was the lost coast of Greenland, which might extend along the Arctic Circle all the way east to the north side of Novaya Zemlya. And who knew where Tabin was, the isthmus or mountain in the far north already mentioned by the Romans, which could prove an obstacle to any northeast passage?

It was a world of uncertainty and fear, of age-old lore compiled by scholars who sifted through works of classical geographers, biblical writers and medieval chroniclers, accounts often based on little more than hearsay. As time passed, the continents on the maps they drew filled up with nonexistent mountains and tribes; the seas acquired imaginary islands, currents, and monsters. Because everything had to be accounted for, and harmonized.

Brunel must have seen these maps—in Louvain, where the renowned mathematician and geographer Gemma Phrysius taught at the university and where Gerard Mercator worked until he grew weary of suspicions of heresy and moved to Duisburg.[34] Brunel had probably read, too, the stories about exotic tribes which German scholars in particular had collected in such impressive numbers, often commissioned by their trade-oriented town councils. And even if he had not read them himself, he certainly would have heard about them and listened eagerly as they were retold. For no one—and certainly no merchant—goes traveling around the world without wondering what he will encounter beyond the horizon.

Only occasionally were there reports from travelers who had seen things with their own eyes: a monk in search of the most tranquil spot on earth, a papal emissary to Russia, a commercial agent like Brunel himself. Their stories seemed thin and colorless compared to the stream of fantasies produced by scholars bent on turning all they had read into a coherent world picture. Gradually, however, eyewitness accounts began to undermine bookish certainties, and toward the end of the century maps were finally being printed with blank areas. Coastlines ended abruptly. At last people knew, and were willing to admit, what they did not know…

---

34   Osley 1969, p. 20-23.

II *The Water*

To return to the beginning: the sky was probably dark and the air damp, with a cold, hard wind blowing from the southwest the day Olivier Brunel rounded North Cape for the first time. And it must have been much the same every time after that. Foggy, with occasional bouts of rain. They sailed close to shore, no more than two miles from the steep cliffs. On their left the sea stretched out far beyond the hazy horizon, where icebergs floated into view now and then like exotic swans.[1] No one knew what a person venturing out there would find…

Far to the north lay the Dead Sea—the ancient Greeks had already claimed to know that much. Birds flying over it would simply fall dead out of the sky. Alexander the Great had been warned about this area when he declared his intention to explore the outermost limits of the inhabited world. The thirty-seven soldiers whom he nevertheless ordered to sail there died as soon as they set foot on board.[2]

Just how much of this was true? Sometime around 330 B.C. Pytheas of Marseilles had set sail for the northern regions with one or two galleys, each carrying about one hundred fifty men. Six days north of England they discovered the island Thule, and one more day of sailing brought them to the frozen sea—known to some as the "Liver Sea"[3]—where the ice was black with age, and where ships were in danger of being enveloped by a "sea lung" of mist and snow, in which sea merged imperceptibly with sky, forcing travelers to wander blindly, lost, to all eternity.[4] No one had really believed this, especially the idea that there was no night there, only an unchanging whitish twilight. That certainly fit the description of the Underworld, but had Pytheas really been there?

It seemed more likely that the earth was encircled by a band of oceans, dotted with egg-shaped islands (see ill. 4). Long after the Greeks had recorded their stories, scholars came to this conclusion on the basis of observed currents and tidal fluctuations. According to Ambrosius Theodosius Macrobius, who lived in North Africa around 400 A.D., two gulf streams split off in both the east and the west from the broad band of water stretching around the earth at the equator. They curved around to the north and the south, and eventually collided with immense force at the poles. Later Paulus

---

1   Veer 1 1917, p. 48; Linschoten 1914, p. 37.
2   Wachsmuth 1967, p. 214-217.
3   Brandaan 1978, p. 72 and 217.
4   Markham 1921, p. 28-29; Hennig 1 1944, p. 154-159; Vaughan 1982, p. 314-315; Dreyer-Eimbcke 1994, p. 132; see also Hennig 2 1950, p. 354.

4.   *World Map* (thirteenth century).
     The world is bounded by a ring of oceans with gulf streams flowing through them.

Diaconus had written that there had to be a giant whirlpool at this point which sucked the streams into the center of the earth twice each day and spewed them out again.[5]

Young Olivier Brunel had certainly heard about all this, if not at school in Louvain, then later in Antwerp where scholarly works lay open to view in bookshops. Too expensive to buy, but who would have refused a young man about to sail north a quick look? Or maybe more than one look?

The one thing to avoid at all cost was to get caught in the gulf stream (see ill. 5). With the speed of an arrow ships would be swept into the abyss, hopelessly lost, although it

5   Verrycken 1990, p. 26, see also illustrations nr. 26 and 27; Macrobius 1952, "Introduction," p. 48-49, and text, p. 200 and 214.

De æstu, fiue fluxu, & refluxu Oceani.

5.   *The Maelstrom.*
     Off the north coast of Norway, between the small island of Röst and the Lofotens, is the
     maelstrom which sucks ships down into the abyss (see also ill. 2).

occasionally happened that the current would suddenly reverse itself and propel them
back out again with the same great force.[6] Countless sailors had experienced this first-
hand, but only a few had lived to tell the story. Adam of Bremen included an account of
a small group of Frisian explorers in his *History of the Archbishopric Hamburg*, written
in the eleventh century at the behest of no other than Archbishop Adalbert.[7]

It happened, he said, in the time of Adalbert's predecessor Alebrand, around the
year 1040. A group of five noblemen had sailed north from East Friesland to see if it
was true that north of the Weser estuary there was no more land to be found, but
only—eventually—frozen sea. After taking an oath of loyalty to one another and to
their venture, they set out in high spirits. They sailed past Denmark, past England, and
after leaving the Orkneys behind them on the left and Norway on the right, they
reached Iceland. From there they journeyed farther north. But somewhere beyond
Greenland and the mysterious Vinland, they found themselves enveloped in thick fog.
Suddenly the ocean started flowing back to its hidden source, pulling the ships along
into the depths at torrential speed. The unfortunate travelers saw that death was imminent. But as they desperately begged God to have mercy on their souls, a countercur-
rent hurled a few of the ships back to a spot far behind the others.

The crews of these rescued ships immediately began rowing with all their might.
Scarcely had they emerged from the fog and ice when an island appeared before them.
The high wall of rocks surrounding it gave it the appearance of a fortress. Once on land,
they found that the inhabitants stayed out of sight in underground caverns, even in the

---

6   Paulus Diaconus 1878, p. 55-56.
7   Toorn-Piebenga 1987, p. 18-19; Dreyer-Eimbcke 1994, p. 133.

middle of the day. At the entrances to their dwellings lay pitchers and bowls made of gold and other precious metals—more than anyone could imagine. They seized as much as they could carry and hurried back toward their ships. Suddenly, however, they saw enormous one-eyed men pursuing them, Cyclopes, with their equally gigantic dogs leading the chase. One of the group was seized, and a split-second later was torn limb from limb before the eyes of his companions. The others, however, managed to reach the ships. They threw their booty inside and rowed away with all the speed they could muster as the giants ran into the sea after them, bellowing with rage.

The survivors returned unharmed to Bremen where they told Bishop Alebrand the full truth of their adventures and presented the precious jugs and bowls, or at least some of them, as an offering to Christ and to the holy father Willehad, the confessor, in gratitude for their safe return.[8]

These men were hardly explorers, of course—pirates would be a more accurate term.[9] Their far-fetched tales probably served to justify their misdeeds, and in view of their costly gifts, Bishop Alebrand had little choice but to believe them. He might, for that matter, have believed them in any case; or he might have been relating a story that he, too, had heard only second-hand. Later, Bishop Adalbert could hardly show disloyalty toward his predecessor, nor would the good canon Adam, in turn, question his superior, Adalbert. Of course Adam further embroidered the story with some choice bits of learning—about Cyclopes, for example—taken from one or the other encyclopedia. But that is not to say he was lying, or simply telling tall tales.[10]

In any case, the report of the gulf stream and the bottomless whirlpool was confirmed many times after that. And not only by the medieval English bishop Giraldus, who was very likely repeating what he had read in books.[11] The mysterious author of the *Inventio Fortunata* (the "Fortunate Discovery") also mentioned it, and although no one knew who this man was, it was generally accepted that he had actually been there. He was said to be a Franciscan monk from Oxford, a mathematician, who had traveled in the northern regions with the aid of an astrolabe he had invented himself, or some similar instrument for determining geographic positions by the stars.[12]

A strange figure he must have cut, with his brown cowl, his bare feet in sandals and the white cord dangling around his waist, as he sailed from island to island, stopping at each new coast to hold his astrolabe at arm's length and stare into the sky. Often, no doubt, he would have to wait for a break in the clouds, with nothing for miles and miles around him but wind and roaring seas. In 1360 this monk was seen at the court of the King of Norway, but after that he faded into the mists of history. Only his book, the *Inventio Fortunata*, remained—or rather the memory of his book, the rumor that someone had seen it once, somewhere, and a reference on a map made in 1508 by Johannes Ruysch.[13] Even Columbus is said to have made efforts to track the book down.[14] It was believed to contain much: about the whirlpool and the four gulf streams

---

8   Adam von Bremen 1917, p. 276-278 (IV.xl).
9   Toorn-Piebenga 1987, p. 26-27.
10   Hennig 1 1944, p. 354-359.
11   Hakluyt 1 1598, p. 122; Macrobius 1952, "Introduction," p. 49.
12   Hakluyt 1 1598, p. 121-122; Oleson 1964, p. 106-107; Durme 1959, nr. 114b, p. 135-138.
13   Nordenskiöld 1889 (1970), p. 57 and 65-66, and plate nr. 32; Burger 1915, p. 263-264.
14   Parry 1968, p. 283.

that were sucked into it, answers to all the many questions raised by the label "Sucking Sea" as found on Ruysch's map.

The gulf stream was not the only danger lurking beyond North Cape, however. The fathomless ocean provided so much space and food that animals of a size unknown anywhere else on earth thrived there. It seemed, too, that the continual churning of the water, the wind, and the currents, brought about a spontaneous generation of strange, and endlessly varied creatures.[15] Saint Brendan, condemned by God to roam the seas, had encountered a crocodile with a mouth more than two meters wide when open, and whole herds of swimming elephants, wild as raging bulls. At one point he and his fellow monks landed on an island covered by forest. Being hungry, they went out to gather wood for a fire. But as they started chopping down a dead tree the entire island plunged under water, forest and all. After a narrow escape they saw from the safety of their small ship that they had set up camp on the back of a giant fish.[16]

These were old stories, of course, from the twelfth century or even earlier. But the renowned Sebastian Münster, professor in Heidelberg and Basel, also wrote about whales which were easily capable of overturning a ship.[17] In his book he had included illustrations from a sea chart of the northern regions published in Venice in 1539 by the brother of the Bishop of Uppsala, Olaus Magnus, also a man of no small reputation. They showed enormous sea horses spewing water and smoke from mouths filled with razor-sharp teeth, fish with scales like armor and jaws like iron-toothed clamps. A sea-serpent coiled itself completely around a ship, and there were lobsters larger than the people they held in the grip of their frightful claws (see ill. 6).[18] Warnings from God, no doubt, to repent and think of the life to come.[19]

But all this was nothing compared to the Magnetic Mountain.[20] The storm that drove Saint Brendan and his companions into the frozen sea seems to have brought them in the vicinity of this threat as well. They had seen ships standing motionless in the sea with only their masts, swaying gently from time to time, still above water. The iron nails in their hulls had drawn them to the Magnetic Mountain, and they would never escape its force.[21]

According to the *Inventio Fortunata* it was located precisely on the North Pole, a gleaming black rock of pure lodestone measuring thirty miles in circumference. Understandable, then, that anything within a wide radius containing even a shred of iron would be drawn to it. Surrounding the mountain was an inland sea shaped like a large barrel, with four openings for water to flow in and out. Upon reaching the Arctic Circle, compasses would stop functioning and ships built with iron nails would be unable to return. At first slowly, but then more and more rapidly, they would be swept along with the current…[22]

---

15 Seneca 2 1974, p. 487. Magnus 1598 (?), p. 276 verso.
16 Brandaan 1978, p. 63-65 and p. 125.
17 Münster 1550 (1968), p. 988-989; Geiger 1886, p. 30.
18 Knauer 1981, p. 49; Nordenskiöld 1889 (1970), p. 59, illus. 32.
19 Knauer 1981, p. 41-44.
20 Hennig 3 1953, p. 319-321.
21 Brandaan 1978, p. 73-75 and 189, commentary p. 217-219; Lecouteux 1984, p. 35 and 48
22 See the map of Ruysch, in Nordenskiöld 1889 (1970), p. 57 and plate nr. 32.

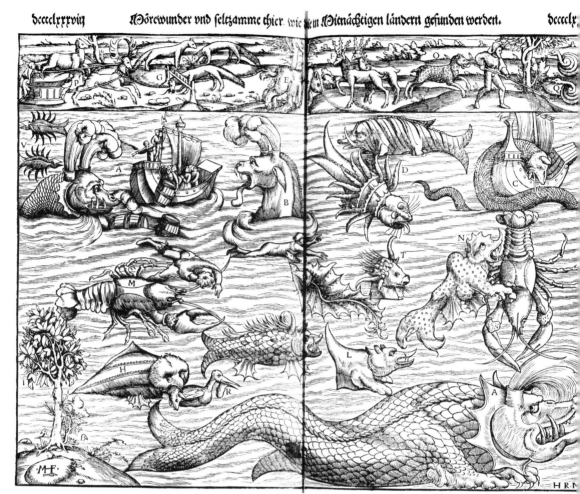

6.   *Sea Monsters in Northern Waters.*

All of these were eyewitness accounts. The seaman overtaken by a storm in those regions had to fear that, once off course, he could be dragged to his doom. He would stare himself blind in the fog, while the sails hung limp and the silence all around was broken only by the occasional sharp cracking of an ice floe. The compass needle was steady. But at any moment it could sweep past north and start spinning, and even if there was still too little wind to turn a flour mill, the ship would start drifting away, unstoppable, despite any desperate efforts to row in the opposite direction. The end would come either as a plunge into fathomless depths or—even more difficult to imagine—a sudden stop followed by a complete inability to move at all.

What, then, was the good of all those rubies and diamonds dotting the seabed, the ones Saint Brendan had seen gleaming in the endless night?[23] God and all his saints

23   Brandaan 1978, p. 91.

would have to protect sailors who ventured too far north, where the devil held sway with his hellish cold and his storms.[24]

What could have motivated a young man like Olivier Brunel to set off for that part of the world from peaceful Louvain, where the sound of prayers rising from dozens of cloisters was broken only by the Latin of scholars and the rowdy antics of students? Desire for wealth, no doubt; insatiable greed. Or worse yet, perhaps, the craving to know what human beings had no right to investigate, a curiosity born of pride. These were the forces that drove him to Antwerp, where the ships with their rounded hulls and high sterns rocked gently at anchor along the wharves of the Schelde.

   – "Looking for something, lad?"
   – "Employment, sir."
   – "Can you read and write?"

Read and write he could, and do arithmetic, and read maps if necessary. And he was not afraid of the devil. So when a ship set sail for the north he was sent along. This would be his chance to find out just how accurate all those maps were, and whether there was indeed only water above North Cape, or land as well, as some maintained.

For maps kept appearing, and in ever increasing numbers since the invention of printing in Germany at the end of the preceding century. Brunel was endlessly fascinated by them: the oldest Ptolemy editions, with their simply sketched coastlines, their handfuls of rivers and mountains and names of tribes; and the later editions with more names, more regions identified, until finally the entire world was full. Whenever he could lay his hands on them he spent breathless hours making comparisons. For ever since the Spanish, Portuguese, and English had begun exploring the seas, no map was identical to the one that preceded it.[25]

   – "Keep your eyes open, lad. Keep your eyes and your ears open. A merchant makes his fortune by watching and listening: new lands, a passage no one knew was there until you discovered it. You have to know a lucky find when you see one, and then seize your chance."

It all began with the discovery of the main work by one of the world's greatest geographers, Claudius Ptolemaeus, of the second century A.D. Unknown in the Middle Ages, his *Geographia*— or *Cosmographia*, as it was also called—had come to light at the beginning of the fifteenth century. Under pressure of the encroaching Turks, the Byzantine Greek empire had finally, after one thousand years of self-imposed isolation, re-established ties with the West. Together with many other texts from Greek antiquity the *Geographia* found its way to Italy, maps and all.[26]

It was a sensation. Countless copies were made of the Latin translation, and the first printed editions soon began appearing as well. They were, to be sure, full of corrections and additions—dozens of them. All over Europe scholars set to work, especially in Italy and Germany, where there were large publishing houses and important trading

---

24 Bächtold-Stäubli 4 1931-32, col. 223-224.
25 See Nordenskiöld 1889 (1970), passim.
26 Verrycken 1990, p.130; Nordenskiöld 1889 (1970), p. 9-10.

7. Claudius Ptolemaeus, *World Map* (1477).
    The outer ring of oceans has disappeared. Where they previously appeared this map sim-
    ply breaks off. In the north this occurs at the sixty-third parallel.

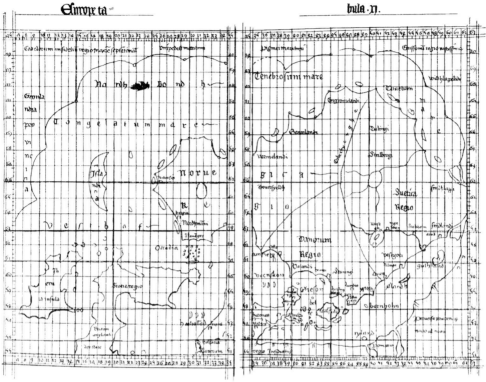

8.   Claudius Clavus, *Scandinavia* (1427).
     The Scandinavian peninsula lies in an east-west direction. Norway, Lapland and part of
     Iceland and Greenland have been added above the sixty-third parallel. Greenland makes a
     large arc above Norway and forms a single continent with Lapland and North Russia.
     One-footed creatures live there ("Unipedi"), as well as Pygmies, Griffins, and Wild Lapps.

companies interested in destinations and distances. Overnight Ptolemy had changed
the picture of the world. The greatest difference between his view and that of the Middle Ages was that he believed the oceans to be inland seas surrounded by land.[27] Gone
was the outer band of oceans, gone were the gulf streams. But gone, too, was the com-
prehensive and—in the most literal sense of the word—well-rounded image of the
earth which was still appearing in textbooks and treatises. Ptolemy's maps simply
stopped at points where they had nothing more to report. The large map of the world
which introduces the collection, for example, breaks off in the north at the sixty-third
parallel (see ill. 7). Beyond Thule, which he placed at this latitude, there was simply no
more world.[28]

---

27   Verrycken 1990, p. 133.
28   Nordenskiöld 1889 (1970), p. 3.

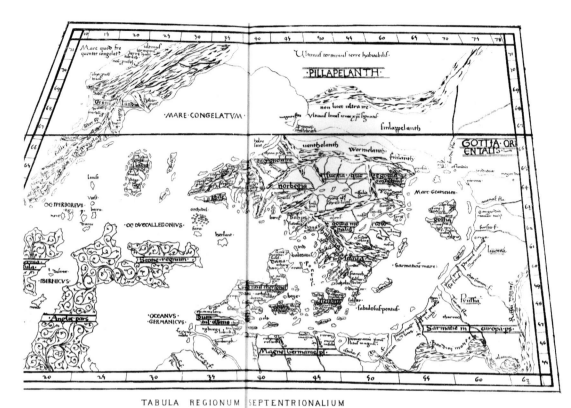

TABULA REGIONUM SEPTENTRIONALIUM

E CODICE PTOLEMÆI SECULI XV. (C. 1467) IN BIBLIOTHECA ZAMOISKIENSI VARSOVIÆ CONSERVATO.

9.   Claudius Ptolemaeus, *The Frozen Sea* ("Mare congelatum") (ca. 1467).
Compared with the map of Claudius Clavus, Finland and the Finn Lapps are situated farther north. The Wild Lapps are here called Pil Lapps.

Scholars racked their brains, trying to decide if this was meant to be "ultima [outer-
most] Thule," in other words Iceland, or the Faroe Islands, or the Orkneys, or even
perhaps Telemark in southern Norway.[29] No one knew the exact location of any of
these places. For Ptolemy, in any case, Thule was an island fairly near the north coast of
England, and Scandinavia an island in the Baltic, directly above the mouth of the Wisla.
East of this estuary the coastline curved sharply to the north. The border of the world
cut straight across northern Russia to some point far above China.[30] No one knew
what lay north of that line. It was a region that had never been visited, and no one had
any desire to go there. So it simply did not exist. At least…

As early as 1427 the Danish geographer Claudius Clavus had recorded, probably
by order of the Danish king, some features of the area above the sixty-third parallel (see
ill. 8). His map shows the entire Scandinavian peninsula, although situated in an east-
west direction, as well as Iceland and, farther to the left, Greenland. In keeping with old
Norse lore found in such works as the thirteenth century *King's Mirror*, written during

29   Verrycken 1990, p. 107; Nordenskiöld 1889 (1970), p. 34, note 1.
30   See for example Ptolemy 1477 (1963), "World Map."

30

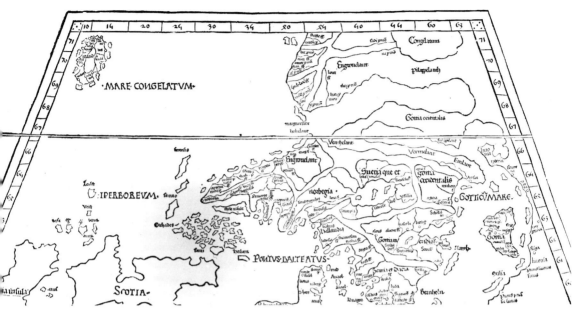

10. Claudius Ptolemaeus, *The Frozen Sea* ("Mare congelatum") (1482).
    Compared with the preceding maps all of Greenland, here called "Engroneland," has been
    moved eastward. It now lies as a second peninsula above Scandinavia, which still extends
    in an east-west direction. Its original location is now occupied by Iceland, which has shift-
    ed from sixty-three to seventy degrees latitude.

the reign of Hakon IV,[31] the coast of Greenland is shown making a wide arc over the
top of Norway and joining Lapland to form a single large continent. The Arctic Sea—
the Frozen, or Dark sea, as it was called—curved around to end as a kind of large bay,
like the Baltic. The polar region itself became a continuous land area inhabited by exotic creatures: Sciapods, Pygmies, Griffins, Wild Lapps.[32] The latter were not to be confused with the Finn Lapps of Finland, who were also shy and savage, but at least
known to be human.[33] Some later maps added, in the new type of round lettering fash-
ionable among scholars, remarks such as, "Farther than this one cannot go," or, behind
a schematically drawn mountain range, "Outermost limit of the inhabited world" (see
ill. 9).[34]

But things kept changing. Owing, perhaps, to the problem of projecting a spherical
body onto a flat surface, or to other factors, Greenland was suddenly shifted to a more
eastward position in the Ptolemy edition published in the German city of Ulm in 1482.
Now it lay not only to the right of Iceland, but even northeast of Norway. Engroneland it is called on this map, and Wild Lapland appears as Pilappeland. Together they

---

31   Vaughan 1982, p. 327-328; Dreyer-Eimbcke 1994, p. 134-135.
32   Nordenskiöld 1889 (1970), p. 49, ill. 27, and p. 54; Hennig 3 1953, p. 322; Okhuizen 1992, p. 11-14.
33   See later in chapter III, p. 49.
34   Nordenskiöld 1889 (1970), plate nr. 30: Ptolemy 1467, "Mare Congelatum."

11. (Illustration page 33.)
    Martin Waldseemüller, *World Map* (1507).
    The first map since the Middle Ages on which the world is ringed by water. Unfortunately the quality of the illustration is poor, but the most important innovations are visible. Greenland is again situated in the west, but the second peninsula of Engroneland is still found above Scandinavia. Both South and North America appear in the extreme west, and in the east Cathay and Zipangu (Japan).

form a kind of second peninsula above, and roughly similar in shape to, Scandinavia. Ice floes rendered it impossible to reach this region by water, and high mountains covered by eternal snow ruled out access by land. Greenlanders were therefore completely cut off from the rest of the world (see ill. 10).[35] Above that, beyond a third dead-end bay, lay a closed arctic continent.[36] Already around the turn of the century, however, this picture was abandoned again in favor of the older medieval idea of a world encircled by oceans.

It must have been contagious—a kind of Columbus syndrome spread over Europe after the Italian explorer returned from his first voyage in 1493. Quite suddenly the ocean came to be viewed as a system of traffic lanes rather than the edge of the world. The Spanish, Portuguese and English kings looked for navigators to send out, and navigators looked for kings who would give them money and charters. Fear of danger was no longer an issue. The pressing question now was not whether there was a gulf stream which might carry people away for good, but whether the passage would be blocked by land.

One of the first maps showing the Ptolemaic world surrounded by water was printed in 1507 by Martin Waldseemüller in the monastery of Saint Dié, about fifty miles from Strasbourg. Waldseemüller had studied in Freiburg and was in contact with humanist circles in Strasbourg and Basel, two leading centers of learning and book production. In the years that followed there would be one Ptolemy edition after another. Waldseemüller was also busy preparing an edition. But the map that would make him famous was published together with the account of Amerigo Vespucci's voyages. It was the first map not only to show all the newly discovered lands in detail, but also to identify them as "America."[37] In the geographical introduction to the book Waldseemüller presented a detailed argument for a world covered by a single ocean containing patches of land.[38] This point was made even more clearly by the map, where dark expanses of water contrasted sharply with white land areas.

It was a splendid map, of gigantic proportions: the world extended across twelve pages, with a combined surface area of three square meters (see ill. 11).[39] In the northwest, at the far side of the black ocean, was a carefully drawn coastline with a strip of white land rising behind it. Inlets were indicated, and dozens of landing points along

35 Herberstein 1984, p. 293.
36 Ptolemy 1482 (1963), "World Map" and "Mare Congelatum;" Sigurdsson 1984, p. 394; Dreyer-Eimbcke 1994, p. 136.
37 Waldseemüller 1907 (1969), "Introduction," p. 1-14.
38 Waldseemüller 1907 (1969), p. 70-71 and p. xxx-xxxi.
39 Waldseemüller 1907 (1969), p. 16.

the coast were identified by name. To the south lay the Caribbean islands, the Gulf of Mexico and South America—as well as a white rectangle containing a few sentences about the discoveries of Columbus. Between Europe and the newly discovered land, bordering all the Northlands of the world, above Iceland and above Greenland there was water. It extended east as well: around the top of the peninsula Engroneland, all the way along the northern coast of Russia to Cathay, just as Marco Polo had reported. There that continent ended, too, with only Japan—or Zipangu, as Polo had called it— occupying a position at the extreme eastern edge of the map comparable to that of America in the west. A white box with text was inserted in the northern area as well, covering half of Engroneland. It related Pliny's story of how a German prince had given to the Roman proconsul Quintus Metellus Celer some men from the Indies who, after being driven off course by a storm somewhere in the far east, had washed ashore on the German coast. This, the text added, could only have happened if there were indeed sea extending all across the north.[40] It was this remark which a few decades later would feed speculation about a northeast passage, an idea which was to take on almost obsessive proportions for more than a century.

So instead of an arctic continent stretching from Greenland to Finland there was water. Waldseemüller's map made its way around the world in no less than a thousand copies. It covered the walls of publishing houses, merchants' offices and town halls. It was also, of course, on display in the monastery of Saint Dié, home of the local human- ist circle, and in the castle of their patron, Duke René of Lorraine. It probably hung as well in one of the many palaces of the Holy Roman Emperor, Maximilian I of Habs- burg. But also in the castles of dukes and princes with intellectual interests throughout the German empire—in Wolfegg, for example, home of the Prince of Waldburg in Würtemberg. And, no doubt, in the city council chambers of Hamburg, Bremen, Lü- beck and other cities with a long-standing interest in seafaring. Soon reprints appeared, as well as smaller-scale copies suited for inclusion in the Ptolemy editions, and—in even greater numbers—adapted and revised versions.[41]

All those maps made one thing clear: there was ocean everywhere, just waiting to be sailed by those who had the courage to go farther than anyone had ever gone before. Not like the medieval monks, who had traveled to the ends of the earth in search of self- denial and solitude, but to acquire riches—tangible, material wealth as seen on the mar- kets of Mecca and Alexandria, and described by travelers like Marco Polo. Spices from the Moluccan Islands, gold from Zipangu, from Cathay. Columbus was also out searching for these things when he stumbled upon America. Those new lands posed a problem, of course, but there had to be a way to sail around them.

- "Keep your eyes open, lad. A sailor with get-up-and-go and an eye for trade and profit can go far in this world, take my word for it."
- "Yes, sir."

---

40   Waldseemüller 1907 (1969), map. See also Burger 1916, p. 37-45; Pliny 1967, p. 304-305 (II. lxvii. 170).
41   Waldseemüller 1907 (1969), "Introduction," p. 3-4 and p. 21-22.

It would not be easy, that much was already clear. According to Brunel's teacher in Louvain, Gemma Phrysius, a Danish or Norwegian navigator named Johannes Scolvuss had already discovered a new tribe, called Quii, in the far western regions of the Arctic Circle in 1476. No one had shown much interest in his reports, although it is quite possible that he, too, had been a brave merchant full of ambitious plans.[42]

In any case, in 1497 there was definitely interest in this sort of enterprise in England. In that year a merchant of Genoese origin and Venetian citizenship, Giovanni Caboto (John Cabot), set sail from Bristol in a northerly direction. Following the example of the Spanish and Portuguese, he hoped to claim new lands for the king of England. He had previously tried in vain to find investors for his plans in Spain and Portugal, possibly in France as well. But in Bristol, the home port of fishermen working the seas around Iceland, ship owners were prepared to listen when he argued that, instead of following Columbus' example, explorers should search for a northern sea route to Cathay and Zipangu. The distance around the earth was shorter at that latitude, and since the trip should not take much longer than one week each way, provisions would not be a problem. As far as the ice was concerned, there seemed little need to worry: the summer days were long in the north, with its low-hanging sun.

Right around this time the English king paid a state visit to Bristol. The court became involved in the planning, and in March of 1496 John Cabot, along with his sons, was granted a charter by Henry VII to sail the seas in an eastward, northward and westward direction, and to take possession of all newly discovered territory where Christians had not yet set foot. In advance he was given the monopoly on trade with those lands, on the condition that it be conducted from Bristol and that one fifth of the profit would go to the king.

The voyage was a success. On June 24, 1497 Cabot reached the North American coast, and after planting the flags of Venice and England, returned to Bristol with the news that he had found the sea route to Asia and Cathay, empire of the Great Khan visited by Marco Polo two centuries earlier.

In both Bristol and London the response was enthusiastic. Armed with maps and a homemade globe to demonstrate his discovery, Cabot went to London where he was received at court. The Spanish ambassador protested to the king that expeditions of this kind infringed on the rights of the Spanish crown. Had not the Pope himself divided the world into Spanish and Portuguese domains immediately following the return of Columbus? But the protest fell on deaf ears.

Italian merchants and envoys relayed news of the success to their contacts at home.[43] Raimondo di Raimondi from Soncino, for example, wrote to his patron, the Duke of Milan, in 1497 about the journey of "Messer Zoane," who had traveled to regions in the far northeast and returned with reports of a temperate climate and a sea so full of fish that simply letting down a basket with a stone inside would yield a fine catch. The concept of a northwest passage was not completely clear to Raimondo, who could only think of Asia in terms of the east. He wrote:

---

42   Hennig 4 1956, p. 248-249 and 261-269.
43   Morison 1978, p. 40-41 and 48-71; Karrow 1993, p. 104.

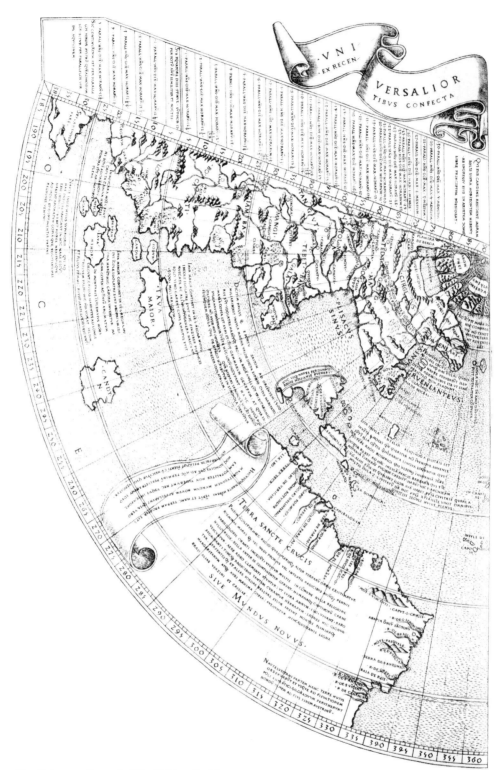

12. Johannes Ruysch, *World Map* (1508).
This is the first map showing the four polar islands, surrounded by mountains. It represents a compromise between the medieval gulf-stream theory and the idea of an arctic continent. The *Inventio Fortunata* is named as the source. The map shows a magnetic moun-

tain at the pole as well as a "sucking sea." The peninsula above Scandinavia is joined to the polar island above it, and Greenland has become part of the North American mainland. There is as yet no separation between North America and Asia.

This Messer Zoane, as a foreigner and a poor man, would not have obtained credence, had it not been that his companions, who are practically all English and from Bristol, testified that he spoke the truth…

These same English, his companions, say that they could bring so many fish that this kingdom would have no further need of Iceland, from which place there comes a very great quantity of fish called stockfish. But Messer Zoane has his mind set upon even greater things, because he proposes to keep along the coast from the place at which he touched, more and more towards the east, until he reaches an island which he calls Cipango, situated in the equinoctial region, where he believes that all the spices of the world have their origin, as well as the jewels. He says that on previous occasions he has been to Mecca, whither spices are borne by caravans from distant countries. When he asked those who brought them what was the place of origin of these spices, they answered that they did not know, but that other caravans came with this merchandise to their homes from distant countries, and these again said that the goods had been brought from other remote regions. He therefore reasons that these things come from places far away from them, and so on from one to the other, always assuming that the earth is round, it follows as a matter of course that the last of all must take them in the north towards the west.

He tells all this in such a way, and makes everything so plain, that I also feel compelled to believe him. What is much more, his Majesty, who is wise and not prodigal, also gives him some credence, because he is giving him fairly good provision, since his return, so Messer Zoane himself tells me. Before very long they say that his Majesty will equip some ships, and in addition he will give them all the malefactors, and they will go to that country and form a colony. By means of this they hope to make London a more important mart for spices than Alexandria. The leading men in this enterprise are from Bristol, and great seamen, and now they know where to go, say that the voyage will not take more than a fortnight, if they have good fortune after leaving Ireland.

I have also spoken with a Burgundian, one of Messer Zoane's companions, who corroborates everything. He wants to go back, because the Admiral, which is the name they give to Messer Zoane, has given him an island. He has given another to his barber, a Genoese by birth, and both consider themselves counts, while my lord the Admiral esteems himself at least a prince.

I also believe that some poor Italian friars will go on this voyage, who have the promise of bishoprics. As I have made friends with the Admiral, I might have an archbishopric if I chose to go there…

Raimondo preferred, however, the secure salary paid by the Duke of Milan, in whose service he made the rounds of dinners and banquets in search of the latest news.[44] But the king and the "men from Bristol" had no trouble financing five ships for a second journey. One of them returned after a short time, but the other four disappeared without a trace.

At a certain point Cabot himself, or his son Sebastian, must have realized their mistake: the coast they had reached was not that of rich Asia but of a vast, sparsely populat-

---

44   Parry 1968, p. 280-282.

12a. Detail from illustration 12.

ed land with scantily clad and, for the most part, hostile inhabitants.[45] It is possible that Sebastian later made a third journey in that direction, although that may have been the same as the second voyage of his father. In any case he maintained that near Newfoundland—which he called Bacalaos (Codfishland)—they had encountered enormous icebergs which prevented them from sailing any farther. Following the coast south from there, he eventually reached Cuba. And nowhere in that endless expanse of new land did he find a passage.[46] But some said that these were all lies, and that he had never been there.[47]

Years later, in any event, long after Sebastian had entered the service of Spain, the account of his presumed voyage appeared in the book about the New World published by Peter Martyr, official historian of the Spanish king. Martyr writes that on several occasions he had invited Cabot to a friendly dinner in his home, since they were colleagues at court. In his opinion, the westward currents observed by Cabot indicated that there must be some movement in the ocean all around the world caused by a cosmic force. But he added, in no uncertain terms, that he did not believe in a whirlpool which was alternately sucked into the earth and spewed out again. Progress had made at least that much clear. He continued: "Now he is waiting, day after day, for ships to be placed at his disposal so that he will be able to unravel this mystery of nature as well."

That was in 1515.[48] Years would pass before this wish was fulfilled, and by then Sebastian was too old to take part in the expedition himself.

---

45   Williamson 1922, p. 70; Morison 1978, p. 72-73.
46   Williamson 1922, p. 71-72.
47   Morison 1978, p. 86-88.
48   Martyr 1 1972, p. 275-276.

13. Orontius Finaeus, *World Map* (1531).
     The polar islands introduced by Ruysch can be seen here, as well as a land connection
     between one of them and the peninsula above Scandinavia. Greenland is separated from
     the American mainland, and the American peninsula jutting eastward is now called
     "Bacalaos." But America and Asia are still not separate continents.

14. Gerard Mercator, *World Map* (1538).
    This early map by Mercator still assumes an Arctic continent, of which Greenland forms a
    part, and which is joined to the European mainland. But the Arctic Strait separates it from
    North America, and Asia and North America no longer form a single land mass.

The voyages of the Cabots—father and son, and possibly one or two other sons—set people thinking once again. Had Ptolemy been right after all, with his idea of an arctic continent?

Some held fast to the idea of an open polar sea, like Robert Thorne, whose father had helped finance Sebastian Cabot and who now had an office of his own in Seville. It was there, no doubt, that the two men became acquainted, after Cabot had entered the service of Spain. In a letter to the English King Henry VIII, as well as in a separate treatise, Thorne made a strong case for a route directly across the pole. There would be some difficulties, of course, as those who had tried it could testify. But another mile or two would certainly have brought them to the pole; it could not be all that cold there, and once beyond that point, they would soon enter a more temperate zone.[49] "So there," he seemed to saying to Cabot.

Others looked for compromise solutions. In 1507 the map made by Johannes Ruysch of Utrecht was published in Rome (see ill. 12).[50] It was the first map to show Cabot's discovery of Bacalaos, which he had named for its inexhaustible quantities of cod, and which he identified with Greenland. It formed a single land mass with the easternmost reaches of Asia; and one would only have to sail around this protruding peninsula in a southwesterly direction to reach Cathay and Kinsai. Japan had disappeared. The Caribbean islands and America lay far to the south, with ocean separating them from Asia.

But in the north Ruysch followed the *Inventio Fortunata*, as he himself noted on the map. With a reference to this source he drew around the arctic area a circular range of high mountains, sliced through by no less than nineteen sea channels. Behind the mountains the waters came together into the four gulf streams, which flowed between four large islands and eventually, in the vicinity of the magnetic mountain, met to form a whirlpool.

Two of the polar islands were believed to be inhabited, one by the Hyperboreans and the other by the Arimpheans, tribes which Pliny had situated somewhere in northeast Russia.[51] The circle of mountains was connected at a few points with the continent of Europe: at the far end of the peninsula Pilapland north of Scandinavia, and by means of two similar isthmuses on the north coast of Asia. Between them lay what the *Inventio Fortunata* evidently prompted him to call the "Sucking Sea," where the gulf stream would pull everything with it, compasses would stop functioning, and ships containing any iron would be unable to move. All this he noted on his map in clear block letters.[52]

Ruysch's view of the four polar islands went unnoticed until it suddenly reappeared in 1531 on a map by Orontius Finaeus, professor of mathematics at the famous Collegium Regium in Paris (see ill. 13), and again much later, in 1569, on the world map of Mercator.[53] For the time being, however, Mercator could proceed from the old fifteenth century idea of a continuous arctic continent which was joined to Europe in northern Russia (see ill. 14). Only above the coast of North America did he draw a passage, the

---

49   Williamson 1922, p. 75; Wallis 1984, p. 453; see also Taylor 1968, p. 46.
50   Bagrow 1964, p. 132 and 269; Kempers 1996, p. 22, 24, 26, 29-30.
51   Pliny 2 1969, p. 362-363 (VI. xiv. 34-35).
52   Nordenskiöld 1889 (1970), plate nr. 32.
53   Nordenskiöld 1889 (1970), plate nr. 41; Mercator 1569 (1961), plate nr. 17; cf. Karrow 1993, p. 378.

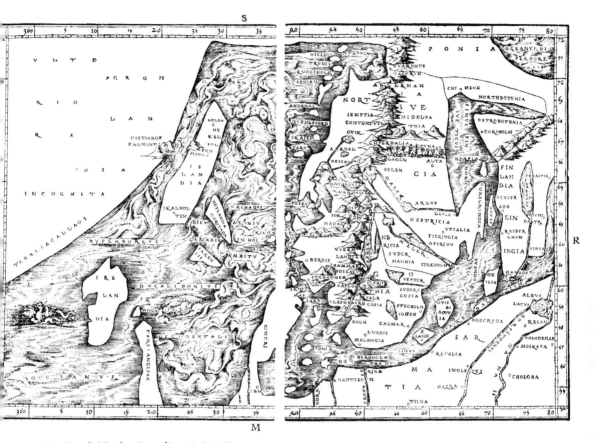

15. Jacob Ziegler, *Scandinavia* (1532).
Greenland is here part of the Arctic continent which extends from North America to Lapland.

Arctic Strait, or as his teacher Gemma Phrysius had called it, the Strait of the Three Brothers—a name believed to refer to the Cabot brothers who had been there on their search for a passage to Asia.[54]

But on this point, too, there was a great deal of disagreement. According to Jacob Ziegler, for example, a German who in 1532 published a book about Scandinavia, the very fact that ice floes had forced Cabot to return proved that the polar land mass extended from Bacalaos to Lapland. Icebergs indicated the presence of land, for the open sea would never be able to freeze, given its salt content and wave motion (see ill. 15).[55]

All these years Sebastian Cabot spent either sailing for the king of Spain—without much success—along the coast of South America, or living at the Spanish court. There he puzzled over theoretical problems, such as the compass deviation observed by Columbus, while feeling annoyed, no doubt, at Ruysch's publication of his own discovery,

54   Nordenskiöld 1889 (1970), plate nr. 43; Skelton 1962, p. 166; cf. Wallis 1984, p. 454; Dreyer-Eimbcke 1994, p.138-140; Van der Krogt 1994, p. 84-85; Hintzsche 1994, p. 176-177.
55   Zieglerus-Krantzius 1583, p. 480; see also Nordenskiöld 1889 (1970), p. 57, ill. 31.

Bacalaos, as well as the irresponsible nonsense propagated by his former compatriot Thorne.

Meanwhile the book by Peter Martyr appeared with Cabot's own travel account, and eventually, in 1544, his map of the world was printed as well. He still rejected the idea that there could be land in the north. But he did note that the sea in that region was completely frozen, for he had seen it himself. Only in the east did he hold open a possibility: the line indicating the north coast of Russia ended abruptly. At this point he added a note about Pliny's story of the Indians, or people from the Indies, who had been driven ashore by a storm at this spot in the time that Quintus Metellus Celer was proconsul of Gaul...[56]

Four years later, in 1548, Cabot, now seventy-three years old, secretly left Spain to place himself in the service of the English king and a group of English merchants. Charles V, King of Spain and the Netherlands, protested against the appointment of a man whom he considered a deserter, and asked the English to send him back. The reply he obtained in 1550 was negative. Eventually, in 1553, everything was ready, and the first expedition of the Merchant Adventurers, the one led by Willoughby, Burrough and Chancellor, set sail. Their instructions had been written by Sebastian Cabot himself. The route was very different from the one he had traveled in his youth. Now the assignment was to sail east, along the north coast of Russia and the lands beyond, and to keep sailing, if possible, until they reached Cathay.[57]

Had he hit on this idea after reading the allusion to Pliny on Waldseemüller's map? Or had he read the description of Russia published in 1525 by Paulus Jovius, based on information from the Russian envoy Dmitri Gerassimov? This book stated plainly that the great river Dvina made a wide arc to the north and eventually flowed into a sea so broad that ships following the coastline could certainly—at least if no land lay in between—reach Cathay.[58]

56   Cabot, Mappemonde 1544 (1968); cf. Karrow 1993, p. 103-112.
57   Williamson 1922, p. 86-88; Coate 1886, p. 166-171; Dreyer-Eimbcke 1994, p.143-146.
58   Jovius-Grynaeus 1532, p. 473; Henning 1906, p. 2; Tracy 1980, p. 6-7.

III *The Land*

Cathay!

The kingdom of Cathay is the largest in the world; it comprises many peoples, and immeasurable wealth and treasures are found there. The people are cleverer and shrewder than anywhere else and surpass all others in the arts and sciences. They maintain, in fact, that they themselves see with two eyes, the Romans with one, and that all other peoples are blind. This is their way of saying that they consider all others uncivilized. But despite their remarkably clear insight into material things, they have not the slightest notion of spiritual matters.

This was how Haithon the Armenian, who eventually lived out his life in a monastery on Cyprus, described Cathay two and a half centuries earlier.[1] By that time the Venetian merchants Niccolò and Maffeo Polo, together with Niccolò's seventeen-year-old son Marco, were already in Peking, where the Khan of all Tartars, Kublai, had established his court. From there he ruled over Tangut and Tenduk, Cathay and Manzi, as well as many other lands both within the borders of old China and outside them. Homesick, however, for the steppes of his childhood, he had ordered wild grass to be planted in the courtyard of his palace, so that among all the silken cushions and highly polished furniture and panels he would not forget the sweat of horses or the fierce cries of warriors galloping over windswept plains.

At that time the caravan routes were still open and travelers—merchants, and before long missionaries as well—were welcome in the empire. But no one stayed there as long or traveled the region as widely as Marco Polo. Between 1275 and 1292 he visited many parts of the realm as a personal envoy of the khan. From Peking he traveled northwest to Cathay, the province which in later writings would bequeath its name to the entire empire.[2]

The climate was pleasant. Roads were well maintained and safe. Travelers could rest and change horses at wayside stations located at regular intervals, and they would never be overtaken by nightfall before reaching the next town. Nowhere were there so many rich, thriving cities to be found so close together.[3]

And nowhere were the marriageable young women so chaste and modest. With good reason, too, for when a father gave his daughter in marriage he had to sign a con-

---

1   Haithon-Grynaeus 1532, p. 367.
2   Polo 1958, p. xii-xv.
3   Polo 1958, p. 134-135.

tract guaranteeing her virginity. The mother and aunts of the bridegroom would verify this with a pigeon egg on the wedding day. That was why they walked so delicately, those girls of Cathay, never putting one foot more than a finger's breadth in front of the other. One careless movement, after all, could have meant the loss of their honor. The Tartars who now ruled the land were not as strict with their wives and daughters. They even rode horses as if they were still on the steppe. Homesick, homesick, like their khan. The old Chinese families watched with disapproval and further tightened the observance of their own traditions as they waited for better times.[4]

Cathay may have had the greatest number of cities, but the richest town of all was found southeast of there in the province of Manzi. This was Kinsai, "City of Heaven," known as the most beautiful city in the world. Polo traveled there as well, and he most likely toured the town by boat. For even though Kinsai was located twenty-five miles inland, the entire city was bounded by a one-hundred-mile ring of water and criss-crossed with canals so broad that ships could moor in front of the houses. There were twelve thousand bridges, with a continual stream of people moving over them, going about their business in the city.

Kinsai was not a city of government officials but of tradesmen and merchants. On ten different market squares, each measuring half a mile on a side, forty to fifty thousand people from far and wide gathered for three days every week to do their buying and selling. Along these squares, from one side of the city to the other, ran a forty-foot-wide thoroughfare, always full of carriages, carts and portable chairs. This artery was also crossed at regular intervals by pedestrian bridges. As for the trades, there were twelve guilds, each with twelve thousand individual workshops where between ten and forty people earned their living.

But whoever was working there, it certainly was not the merchants or the owners of the businesses themselves, or even the supervisors. Nowhere did people enjoy recreation so much, and nowhere could they afford it so well. There were more than three thousand bathhouses for both men and women. And scattered through the city were the luxurious apartments of courtesans, all splendidly dressed and perfumed, and so skilled in the arts of pleasing and caressing that for this reason alone foreigners would later remember Kinsai as a city of heaven.

Those living there, rich and poor alike, found their greatest enjoyment in boating on the large lake south of the city. Palaces and country houses of the rich lined the shore, as well as monasteries. On each of two islands in the middle of the lake stood a magnificent building with so many rooms and apartments that it resembled the palace of an emperor. Here weddings and other festivities were celebrated, banquets for over one hundred people, and several of them could take place at the same time without interfering with one another. On the lake itself were a large number of boats, big and small, offering pleasure trips for groups of ten, fifteen, twenty or more. Anyone wishing to relax on the lake with his female companions could rent one. They came complete with a protective roof, benches with soft cushions, and everything else one might desire. It was a scene of colorful confusion, with music wafting over the water and passengers in one boat waving to those in others. Nothing gave the residents of Kinsai more pleasure after finishing their work than to spend part of the day here with their wives or hired

---

4   Polo 1958, p. 167-169.

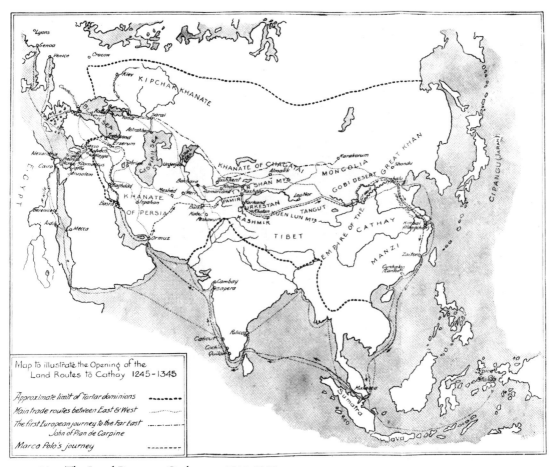

16. *The Land Routes to Cathay*, ca. 1245-1345.
   In the age of the Tartars there was relatively intense trading between Europe and China.
   This was cut off by the rise of the Ottoman Empire.

women, to go boating, or to take a carriage ride to one of the public gardens in the area where they would be received by the park wardens in arbors set up specially for this purpose, and where they would stay till late in the evening.

So rich were these people and so profitable their trade that according to Marco Polo's reckoning the Great Khan received no less than fourteen million seven hundred thousand pieces of gold per year from Kinsai and its dependent cities alone.[5] So rich was Cathay. All this had been dictated by Marco Polo himself after his return to Italy at the end of the thirteenth century.[6]

---

5   Polo 1958, p. 184-193 and p. 201.
6   Verrycken 1990, p. 151.

By the time Olivier Brunel crossed the Urals sometime at the end of the 1560's or the beginning of the 1570's, and heard in the city of Yaks Olgush, as he later claimed, about richly laden ships coming from a land somewhere in the east, Polo's story was a well-established myth. A dream about a way of life imaginable only in heaven, not in the cold reality of Antwerp, and certainly not in Moscow, where Anthony Jenkinson boasted about the trips he had made to Persia by way of Kazan' and Astrakhan ten years earlier. All the wealth of the Persian throne would be nothing compared to that of Cathay.[7]

But no one had traveled that far east for over two centuries. Less than fifty years after Marco Polo's return to Italy, the traditional caravan routes—by way of Akko and Baghdad, then along the Sea of Azov to Astrakhan and straight across Turkestan to China (see ill. 16)—had been cut off by the Ottoman Moslems.[8] Appearing out of nowhere they had within the shortest possible time conquered first Asia Minor, then parts of Europe as well. The half moon and the scimitar now ruled over Bulgaria, Serbia, Greece and, most recently, Hungary and parts of Austria. By 1529 they had even reached the gates of Vienna, and the danger that they would not stop there was still very real.[9]

Goods found their way through nevertheless—silk, precious stones, the resin of aloes—and along with them stories kept coming as well. There must have been many travelers like Giovanni Caboto, who heard the tales from caravan guides in Mecca. But direct trade was no longer possible. Goods were sold and transferred from one caravan to another, with the prices rising at every border, much to the satisfaction of the Turkish toll collectors and the Arabian traders. When they finally reached the markets of the west the quantities were minimal and the prices exorbitant.

Everyone knew that the person who could find a way to re-establish the direct connection would make staggering profits. Christopher Columbus had known this, but he had run up against troublesome America where the natives ran naked and one had to pay dearly in blood and sweat for whatever silver could be found. And Vasco da Gama had known it when he rounded the Cape of Good Hope, but he never got farther than India. Sebastian Cabot knew it, too, and Burrough, toiling through the ice of Novaya Zemlya, and Jenkinson no doubt.

But how was one to get there? The geographers suggested one possibility after another: a northwestern route, a northeastern route or even directly over the pole. Discussions very likely took place in the offices of Gillis Hooftman, or in the workshop of the cartographer Abraham Ortelius, whose atlas was said to have been financed by Hooftman himself.[10]

- "Through Russia, perhaps, and on through Central Asia?"
- "Jenkinson says that's not possible because of the bloodythirsty tribes there—it's all anarchy and endless war." [11]
- "I mean a more northern route."

---

7   Purchas 12 1906, p. 1-54; Karrow 1993, p. 317-318.
8   Cipolla 1973, p. 277-280; Power 1968, p. 143.
9   Roux 1985, p. 225-308.
10   Ortelius 1570 (1964), p. v-vi.
11   Williamson 1922, p. 114; Willan 1959, p. 153.

- "More northern? That would bring you through the empire of the Antichrist."
- "Really, now…"
- "What do the Scriptures tell us about Gog from the land of Magog, the chief prince of Mesech and Tubal? Read Ezekiel 38:15-19: 'they'll come from the north, they and many peoples with them. They will all be riding on horses, a mighty army. And there will be a great shaking…'"
- "But really…"
- "In Revelations 20:7-9 it says that at the end of the thousand-year reign, Satan will be released from captivity and will go to deceive the peoples of Gog and Magog and gather them together for war, and they will spread over the earth like the sands of the seashore."
- "At the end of the thousand-year reign—we're not anywhere near that yet. Let it begin first."
- "Mock all you like, you don't know what you're talking about… Anyway, everyone knows that when Alexander the Great traveled to the ends of the earth he imprisoned all the barbarians living in the far north behind an enormous wall. Who could that have been besides Gog and Magog? Maps made hundreds of years ago show these names with a wall drawn around them.[12] Do you think you know more than the best scholars? Martin Waldseemüller says they are actually the ten lost tribes of Israel, the ones that were never heard of again after the Persian king Artaxerxes sent them into exile. And many scholars agree with him."[13]
- "There is nothing about all that on Ptolemy's maps, though."
- "On Ptolemy's maps you find the Scythians, the Anthropophagi and Hippophagi or Hippopedi, instead of Gog and Magog, just as you find "Land of the Chinese" instead of Cathay and Manzi.[14] The names don't always have to be the same. Marco Polo was there himself, remember, and he writes that they are now called Ung and Mungul. The Gog, he says, live in Ung, and the Tartars or Mongols in Mungul.[15] For Johannes Ruysch, in any case, that was reason enough to give a place on his map not only to Cathay, Kinsai and Manzi but also to put Gog and Magog between Waldseemüller's 'Judei inclusi' and Cathay" (see ill. 12).[16]
- "Oh, but Johannes Ruysch put so much on that map. And it's doubtful whether he really existed at all. Nobody knows who he was."
- "The north is dangerous, that much we know for sure, too dangerous for any human being to venture out there. It's the kingdom of Satan and of eternal darkness. Sorcery, black magic. No mortal returns from there alive. Think of what the prophet Jeremiah said: 'evil will come out of the north and spread over the earth.'"[17]

---

12   Verrycken 1990, p. 100-105; Janssens-Uyttersprot 1990, p. 95.
13   Waldseemüller 1907 (1969), map; Verrycken 1990, p. 104.
14   See, for example, Ptolemy 1477 (1963), "World Map" and "Scithia extra imaum montem."
15   Polo 1958, p. xxiii and p. 76.
16   Nordenskiöld 1889 (1970), plate nr. 32.
17   Bächtold-Stäubli 4 1931-32, col. 223; Jeremiah 1:13-14, 4:6, 6:1, 47:2, 50:3, 51:48.

From the earliest Middle Ages the Goths had been considered the sons of Magog.[18] But after the Mongols made their way across Asia and expanded their power as far as Peking, it became clear that these were really the people of Gog and Magog, and the same as the ten lost tribes of Israel. This idea can already be found in the mid-thirteenth century writings of William of Rubruck, who had visited these regions as an envoy of the French king, and soon after that in the work of Marco Polo himself.[19]

But it was only in this century, as scholars started taking a fresh look at the Holy Scriptures and the works of the church fathers, and as some even gained access to mystical Jewish writings, that certain things were becoming clear… This was especially true here in Antwerp, where some of the greatest minds frequented Ortelius' workshop and Plantijn's printery, serious men for whom even Hebrew held no secrets, and who could confidently open the heavy folio editions and point to authoritative passages. There was Benito Arias Montano, emissary of Philip II himself, and, it was rumored, the great hermetic scholar Guillaume Postel.[20] As a result medieval travel writing gradually came to be taken more seriously again.

The only question was whether a merchant, no matter how pious he might be, should be deterred by such considerations. It might all be true, but business was business, and with a pocket full of money things would undoubtedly fall into place there as well. As for the last days...once they were here no one who was not counted among the righteous would be safe anyway, for that one really did not have to avoid going north. Overland then, straight across the north of Asia. That is to say, first by sea past North Cape and along the south coast of Novaya Zemlya into the Kara Sea, and on to the mouth of the Ob'. But from there inland by sailing up the Ob'. This must have seemed the most promising route in those years. Later, in the 1580's, it would be mentioned in the instructions written for Pet and Jackman, and Mercator would recommend it in his letter to Hakluyt. But the idea must have come up already around 1570, when Ortelius included in his world atlas a map of Tartary which showed the coastline beyond the Ob' curving so sharply to the north that sailing any farther along the north coast of Russia—the plan Cabot must have had in mind—was simply out of the question (see ill. 28).[21]

There were dangers enough, of course, even without the Antichrist. Just reaching the Ob' was no simple matter, with the fog and the ice floes, especially around Novaya Zemlya, and with those bloodthirsty natives working all sorts of magic. But the real problems came after that. All that anyone knew about the route to be taken from the Ob' estuary was the account which the German diplomat Siegmund von Herberstein had found in Moscow and subsequently published in his book about Russia.

According to that source—but where did it come from and how reliable was it?—the Ob' originated in the Lake of Kittay, which was situated in, or at least near, China or Cathay. From there, it said, "black people" traveled down the river with a wide variety of goods, especially pearls and precious stones, which they sold to the Tartars living along the way. And they bought the hides which the Tartars, in turn, had acquired from the Lucomories, a people living in the mountains of the north, near the Ob' estuary. Of

18   Borst 2.1 1958, p. 428-429 and 446-453.
19   Verrycken 1990, p. 161-163; Purchas 11 1906, p. 160 and 163-165.
20   Rekers 1961, p. 23-30 and p. 107-110.
21   Ortelius 1570 (1964), map 47 "Tartaria."

them it was said that once every year—on the twenty-seventh of November, the day the Russians celebrate the birth of St. Gregory—they died, and that they were then reborn in the spring, on the twenty-fourth day of April. So shy they were that when the time came for them to die, they simply left their wares at a designated spot and disappeared. The Tartars would then come and take them away, leaving in their place goods of equal value. But if the Lucomories, upon coming to life again in the spring, noticed that they had not been left the correct amounts, there was war. And fight they could, even the Tartars respected them for that.[22]

Von Herberstein's book lay on the table in Ortelius' workshop, and the Lake of Kittay appeared on his map of Tartary.[23] But this was nothing new for Brunel, who had heard similar stories in Yaks Olgush. The question was simply how far it was, and how many tribes and peoples, besides the Lucomories and the Tartars, one would encounter before reaching the source of the Ob'. And after that. For Ortelius' map differed from Von Herberstein's reports in showing vast new lands stretching between Lake Kittay and China, or Cathay.

The classical authors had known this already. Ptolemy's large map of the northern hemisphere, produced by a conical projection which yielded a reasonably close correspondence to actual distances, made it clear that a traveler starting from the coast would have to cross one mountain range after another. Like delicate streamers they stretched over white plains broken here and there by a dotted line for a river or by a name of a tribe. First came the Ripaean Mountains, which ran from south to north, up to the point where the great Alexander had erected his altar and, a short distance farther, two pillars to mark the border of the inhabited world. North of that, running east-west, were the Hyperborean Mountains. In the regions above them lived the Hyperboreans, and south of them, between the Ripaean and the Imaus Mountains far to the east, the Scythians. And beyond the Imaus range were more Scythians.[24]

So many peoples and tribes (see ill. 17). Pliny had written about them, as had Pomponius Mela and later, in the third century, Caius Julius Solinus, whose work had recently been published by Plantijn in Antwerp. To say nothing of all the writers who had added details of their own in the following centuries. They had obtained their information from soldiers who had accompanied Alexander the Great on his campaigns to conquer the world, as well as from captive barbarians and from travelers, men with flat faces and straight black hair who had come from distant lands, and who told stories about places even farther away.

According to Pliny, the Ripaean Mountains ended in a region of deep darkness and eternal frost, where the north wind reigned supreme and snow fell like feathers. Beyond that, he maintained, even farther north, was the home of the Hyperboreans, happy creatures who lived longer than anyone else on earth.

How often had young Olivier Brunel read that text, after tracing the letters with his finger for the first time in the stuffy classroom, stumbling from word to word in his translation and occasionally getting lost in the Latin constructions:

---

22   Herberstein 1557, p. 88 recto-89 recto; Henning 1906, p. 17-19; Tracy 1980, p. 9-10.
23   Ortelius 1570 (1964), map 47 "Tartaria;" Bagrow 1962, p. 45; Okhuizen 1992, p. 18.
24   See for example Ptolemy 1477 (1963), "World Map;" Hennig 1 1944, p. 183.

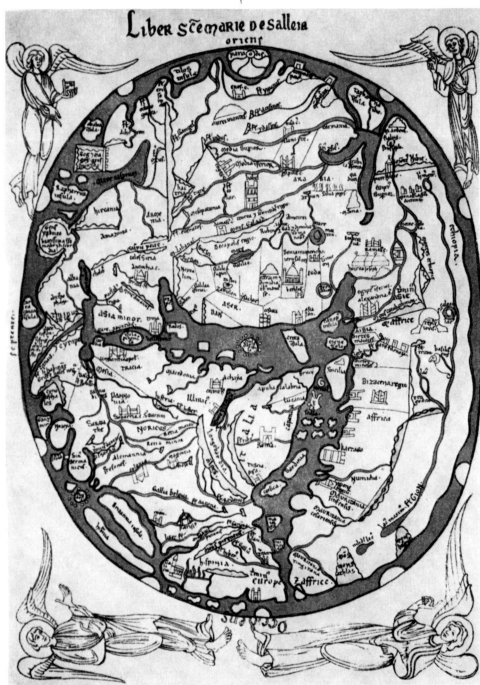

17. Heinrich von Mainz, *World Map* (twelfth century).
     Various mythical peoples are shown as inhabiting the north: Cynocephali (dog-headed
     people), Anthropophagi (cannibals), Amazons, Hyperboreans, and Gog and Magog.

Here are believed to be the hinges on which the firmament turns and the extreme limits of the revolutions of the stars…: for these people the sun rises once in the year, at midsummer, and sets once, at midwinter. It is a genial region, with a delightful climate and exempt from every harmful blast. The homes of the natives are the woods and groves…; all discord and sorrow is unknown. Death comes to them only when, owing to satiety of life, after holding a banquet and anointing their old age with luxury, they leap from a certain rock into the sea…

In a region having six months of daylight… they sow in the morning periods, reap at midday, pluck the fruit from the trees at sunset, and retire into caves for the night… They regularly send the first fruits of their harvests to Delos as offerings to Apollo, whom they specially worship. These offerings used to be brought by virgins, who for many years were held in veneration and hospitably entertained by the nations on the route, until, because of a violation of good faith they instituted the custom of depositing their offerings at the nearest frontier of their neighbouring people, and these of passing them on to their neighbours, and so till they finally reached Delos. Later this practice itself also passed out of use.[25]

Later, when he was in the service of the Stroganovs, this passage from Pliny must have kept echoing in his mind as he listened to stories about the Lucomories or the Samoyeds.

The region on the far side of the Ripaean Mountains was said to be uninhabited but rich in gold and precious stones, especially emerald and crystal. These treasures were guarded by griffins, the fiercest birds on earth; half lion and half eagle, they would swoop down and devour anyone they spotted from their lookout high on the rocks.[26] Most of the regions, however, were inhabited by one tribe or another.

East of the Hyperboreans lived the Arimpheans, a peaceful people who considered long hair disgraceful, for both men and women. Then came the Amazons. The territory of this female tribe extended all the way south to the Caspian Sea.[27] It was said that they became pregnant from a swallow of water, although it was more likely the doing of passing merchants, or of prisoners whom they captured in their raids and carried off for the purpose of providing progeny.[28] Or of the monsters frequently encountered in those regions: people with their heads in their chests, who barked more than they spoke—they had been seen as prisoners in Russia. There were stories about the Amazons' annual festivities, after which they chased the men away again. Male infants they did not keep either, but later sent them to their fathers.[29] They were far from being the strangest tribe which the books described, however.

Beyond the Amazons lived the Scythians, who kept their children hidden deep in forests and caves until they were able to jump from the rocks when being pursued. With their sharp ears they could hear every sound. Like dogs they barked and always ran against the wind so that their scent would stay behind them.[30] They were divided into

---

25   Pliny 2 1969, p. 186-189 (IV. xii. 88-91).
26   Solinus 1572, p. 116; Franck 1595, p. 53 recto.
27   Pliny 2 1969, p. 362-363 (VI. xiv. 34-35).
28   Adam von Bremen 1917, p. 246-248 (IV. xix.)
29   Franck 1595, p. 53 recto.
30   Solinus 1572, p. 124 (xxii).

countless tribes, one more bloodthirsty than the other: the Massagetae and Arimaspi, who had just one eye and who were constantly at war with the griffins over the gold.[31] There were the Neuri as well, who changed into wolves every summer and became human again in the winter; they worshipped their swords instead of images and burned the bones of their prisoners on their altars. And the Gelones, who stripped the skin from their enemies' bodies. After making a slit around the skull and along the arms and fingers, they would pull the skin off in one piece. The scalp with hair they would put on their own head and allow the rest to hang loosely from their shoulders. Or they would cut from it caparisons and other ornamental gear for their horses. And there were the Agathysians, who dyed themselves blue—the higher their rank the deeper the blue. Farther along came the Albans, who believed they were the descendants of Jason himself, and who were born with white hair and eyes of fire with which they could see better by night than by day. They were said to have gigantic dogs, more savage than any wild animal; their fearful bark was louder than the roar of a lion, and they could tear even wild bulls to pieces.[32]

Farther east yet, beyond the Imaus Mountains, came the Scythian tribe of cannibals, the Anthropophagi. Since everyone gave them a wide berth, the surrounding areas were uninhabited and desolate. Only wild animals lived there and they, too, were waiting to pounce on people and tear them apart.[33] Probably the most barbarous of all were the Essedones, who would sing decorously as they followed the funeral processions of their kinsmen, but then tear the corpses apart with their teeth and cook the flesh together with animal meat for a festive banquet. From the skulls they made gold-plated drinking vessels, a practice also common among other Scythians, although they used only the skulls of their enemies. For when a Scythian killed someone he drank his victim's blood and brought his head to the king as proof of his valor. Anyone who had not killed a man for an entire year was considered dishonorable.[34]

Finally, after the last Scythians and the empty regions surrounding them, came the Isthmus of Tabin, which according to Pliny and other writers extended far north from there, almost to the pole. And only then—after a thirteen-day journey over more vast plains, which Marco Polo described as dotted with lakes and marshes and so muddy from ice water that horses were unable to walk there—only then would a traveler catch sight of Cathay.[35]

All those Scythian tribes were eventually conquered by the equally bloodthirsty Tartars, a hideous people with bulging eyes, bushy eyebrows and a loud, strident language which no one could understand. They were always on horseback, their women and children as well. Although not the worst of cannibals, they too ate their enemies, and the story went that whoever did so in the most wolfish way was considered the most heroic.[36] Everyone living in those regions was, after all, under the influence of Aquarius

---

31   Pliny 2 1969, p. 374-375 (VI. xix. 50) and 512-513 (VII. ii. 10).
32   Solinus 1572, p. 111-113 (xx).
33   Pliny 2 1969, p. 376-377 (VI. xx. 53)
34   Solinus 1572, p. 114-115 (xx); Franck 1595, p. 53 verso.
35   Pliny 2 1969, p. 378-379 (VI. xx. 53-54); Polo 1958, p. 304-305.
36   Franck 1595, p. 55 recto.

and Saturn, and these were known to produce the most vicious and belligerent personality traits.[37] So the story went.

In any case, they were formidable fighters. In the past, one year after a gigantic comet had stretched its tail far into the west and circled over Russia for eighteen days in the month of May, in the year 1211 to be exact, they swept into Europe with their wild hordes, destroying everything they found in their path, in blind obedience to their chiefs, the khans.[38] Stories were still being told which kept this fear alive. But now they stayed in the area behind the Urals, where they wandered with their immense herds from the steppes in the south to the tundras in the north. They were known, above all, for their thirst for gold, which meant that a traveler with a saddlebag full of gold coins would never ask in vain for a piece of meat or a cup of milk. As long as he kept his fire burning at night and slept with one eye open, that is, for thieves they were, and that they would remain.

Brunel knew them well from his trips to the Irtysh and the Ob'. He had visited their chieftains in their pointed tents and inspected the hides which they offered to sell him. And while haggling over the price he had looked around and casually asked a few questions: how far in the direction of the North Star—which they called Selesnikol, the Iron Nail—was it to the horde of the Baschirdoi, and from there to the Chiesani, and from there to the Usezucani, to the Ciremissi and whatever all those other tribes or hordes were called.[39] He was hoping to find out how far the land extended north, and whether Tabin might be found up there, the isthmus which would inevitably block the way of any ship sailing to the far east along the northern coast of Russia. Question after question he asked: from whom had they bought the hides, and the precious stones which they showed him; and were there ships that came down the river, rowed by men with skin even darker than theirs?

For if one thing was clear it was that any transport of goods from Cathay had to take place by ship. Either along the northern coast, if it did not curve so far to the north that ice would rule out all possibility of a passage, or by way of the rivers. Even if one had no fear of the Tartars attacking, a danger already pointed out by Jenkinson, an overland route was still inconceivable. For how could goods be dragged over unpaved tracks, with no wayside stations offering fresh camels and mules or food and drink for the next stage of the journey? By ship it would be relatively easy and safe. Then it would not matter if some descendants of the old Scythian tribes with their barbarous customs were still living in a few remote areas, Gog and Magog for example; or if the far north or east were home to the monsters described in books: Cyclops with one eye in their foreheads, the Dog-headed people, and the headless Blemmyae with their eyes, noses and mouths in their chests, or the Ymantopedes, creatures who jumped around on one gigantic foot, or the ones who had no feet at all and depended on their extraordinarily long arms and hands to move from one place to another (see ill. 18).[40] As late as 1540 Sebastian Münster had included pictures of them in his Ptolemy edition.[41] And even if it was clear that he thought of them as remnants of outdated superstition, one

---

37   Michov-Grynaeus 1532, p. 437.
38   Michov-Grynaeus 1532, p. 424-425.
39   Ortelius 1571, page 47 "Tartaria;" Ortelius 1570 (1974), page and map 47 "Tartaria."
40   Adam von Bremen 1917, p. 247-248 (IV. xix) and p. 256-257 (IV. xxv).
41   Ptolemy 1540 (1966), "Tabulae Asiae VIII," "Scythia extra Imaum."

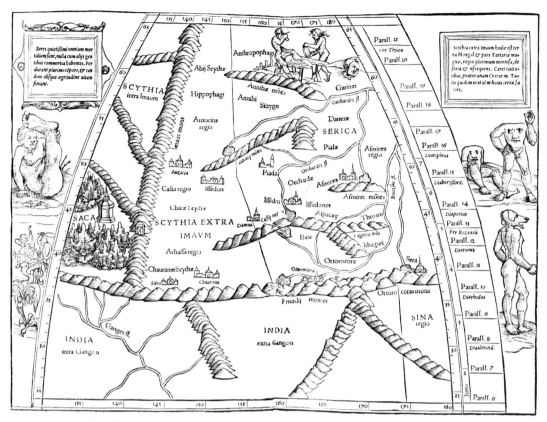

18. Claudius Ptolemaeus, Sebastian Münster, *Scythia Beyond the Imaus* (1540).
    The far east in particular was thought to be the home of mysterious and often violent peoples: Ymantopedes (one-footed creatures), Anthropophagi (Cannibals), the headless Blemmyae and the Cynocephali (dog-headed people).

could never be sure. Truth was often stranger than the most extravagant fiction, and as long as no one knew for certain…

One person who had no patience for all those stories was Mathias of Michov, the learned canon of Cracow. A strong-willed and stubborn man, no doubt, he had given up his position as physician at the court of the Polish king to become a monk; used his wealth to found hospitals and schools; and challenged the authority of some of the most famous scholars from antiquity onwards, relying on nothing more than his own observation.[42] And what could be more certain than personal observation?

–   "Take it from me, my good man, you can trust your own senses, even if they did take you blindfolded all the way from Kholmogory to Yaroslavl'. The Ripaean Mountains simply do not exist, and there is no such thing as the Hyperborean range either. Ha, ha, even blindfolded you saw it better than all those educated cosmographers who use all their clever arguments to string fantasies together."

–   "Then what do you think the landscape is like?"

–   "Rocky, with rolling hills. And forests, endless impenetrable forests; they go on and on, several days' journey to the north and even farther to the east."

–   "But if they're impenetrable, no one can say what might be found in there?"

–   "True, true, but in any case no gold or silver or precious stones, otherwise people would have been there long ago, impenetrable or not. Ha, ha. And certainly no griffins so strong that they can carry a horse off into the sky. At most a golden eagle, maybe a small dragon or two. There are no such things as griffins. Just as there are no monstrous creatures with dogs' heads, rabbits' heads, two heads, no heads, you name it. Good bedtime stories, but in a cosmography... Ah, my lad, there's no limit to what you can put on paper, and scholars are even more vain than the rest of humanity. They're always trying to come up with something spectacular, believe me. Elysian fields where the climate is always mild and the people end their long and happy lives by plunging contentedly into the sea. Ha, ha, and in the north, no less. As if everybody didn't cling to life like a ship-wrecked sailor to a floating barrel. There really is nothing more to be found up there in the north than a few pathetic creatures, living in underground caverns deep in those miserable forests and eating raw fish and the raw flesh of wild animals."[43]

–   "The Lapps?"

–   " 'Lapps' is a name they don't use, because it means 'fools' or 'stupid ones.'[44] And they are certainly not stupid. Long ago they were called Skrittfinns, for the jumps they made on those ashwood slats they glide on, steering themselves with a pole as they hunt game (see ill. 19). One slat is a foot longer than the other; they say this makes for better gliding; and the shorter of the two has to be just as long as the man or woman wearing them is tall. At the front they curve upward, and the underside is covered with reindeer hide—which makes it easier to turn and also keeps them from sliding back down a steep incline. Resistance from the hairs on the hide, understand? I've seen for myself how they swoop down the slopes, racing deep into the mountains with wide, swinging curves, going up as fast as they came down. No matter how suddenly an obstacle turns up in their path, one sharp turn brings them safely around it. Sometimes they do this for no other reason than to see who is the fastest."[45]

–   "The fastest? You mean not because they're out chasing game or something?"

–   "Just for fun. It looks so easy, you almost feel like trying it yourself."

–   "Strange fun. And you say they're not foolish? Where do they come from?"

42   *Nouvelle biographie générale* 35 1861, col. 458; Michow 1906, p. 13.
43   Michov-Grynaeus 1532, p. 423 and p. 446-447.
44   Münster 1550 (1968), p. 986.

Adhuc de situ, & qualitatibus eius.

19. *Lapps.*
The Lapps move like lightning on their skis and in their reindeer-drawn sleighs.

- "Actually, all the people from Kola to Novaya Zemlya belong to the Iuhri, a tribe of Scythians who drove out the Goths who lived there originally."
- "The same Goths who eventually conquered Italy and Spain?"
- "That's right. And the same Iuhri as the people known as Hungarians in the south."
- "The same? How can that be?"
- "On the run from the Tartars, lad, they split up, one part went north and the other south. All the tribes were on the move. You wouldn't believe the havoc those hordes created."[46]

Just how much of this was true remained to be seen. But as far as the Iuhri were concerned, Father Mathias was right about them being a shy people without any higher culture. They could not survive without snow, unbelievable as that might seem.[47] And they did indeed live on the raw flesh of wild animals, clothe themselves in animal skins and wander from place to place with their tents, never settling anywhere permanently. They had no horses, but they did use a kind of deer to pull their sleighs in which they could travel up to one hundred fifty miles per day, a distance they described as three

45   Saxo 1 1979, p. 9 and 2 1980, p. 24; Magnus 1558, p. 2 recto-verso.
46   Michov-Grynaeus 1532, p. 437.
47   Adam von Bremen 1917, p. 266 (IV. xxxii).

20. *Lapps.*
They live by hunting and fishing and they worship statues carved from wood.

changes of the horizon (see ill. 20). This meant that at three different times they could see in the distance another marker erected along the way. Or they streaked along the wild rivers in little boats made of twigs tied together with thongs. And while the Ethiopians dried their fish in the sun, they dried them in the cold, then pulverized them into a kind of meal.

As was to be expected of a wild people who had never been in contact with civilization, their customs were strange. It was forbidden, for example, for a woman to leave the tent by the same opening which her husband had used to go out hunting for the day. Nor was she allowed to touch the dead game with her hands; instead her husband would present her with as much meat as he saw fit to give her from the point of his spear. They were extremely superstitious and had erected images in the mountains which they believed to be gods.[48] Or rather, upright stones roughly resembling human figures, sprinkled with blood, and in some cases, simple pieces of wood with two or three holes in them for eyes and a nose. In front of them they would recite their magic incantations.[49] They worshipped the sun, moon, and stars. Or they would hang a piece of red cloth on a stick and worship that, because the color of blood for them indicated the presence of a god. They made burnt offerings from the bones of walruses and other wild animals, but not in the summer, for then they might appear to be mocking the heat of the sun with their fires. They saved up all the bones until the dead of winter, then made an enormous blaze that lit up the area all the way to the horizon, making it seem as if the sun had returned.[50] To a certain extent this was all understandable—no reason to fear. But there were also stories about how skilled they were at magic and sorcery.

Adam of Bremen had already mentioned how they boasted of knowing everything that happened all over the world.[51] And later Saxo, the historian of the Danish kings, described their fighting tactic of throwing little stones behind them which their enemies perceived as mountains, or handfuls of snow which looked to their pursuers like broad rivers obstructing their path.[52] Those writers were from the Dark Ages. But a contemporary scholar like Jakob Ziegler, who had taught in universities all over Germany and Hungary, also wrote about the spells which they would sing to charm whales to the shore, and about the straps with three knots in which they held the winds captive. By loosening one knot they would start a gentle breeze, two undone would bring a stronger wind, and untying the third unleashed a storm so violent that any seaman who escaped with his life could consider himself lucky. With their arts they could bring ships to a halt in the middle of the sea, with no way to start them moving again.[53] The only protection was to coat a ship inside and out with the excrement of young virgins.[54]

It was known that they could see the future in fire and crystal, and above all, that they were dangerous. When out for revenge they could shoot and hit their enemies from any distance with short magic arrows made of lead, no longer than a finger. Their victims would suffer horrible pain and die within three days of cancer in their arms and legs.[55] All in all, one could say that they had mastered all the devilish arts which the Scriptures had forbidden.

---

48   Zieglerus-Krantzius 1583, p. 481-482.
49   Hakluyt 1 1598, p. 281.
50   Magnus 1558, p. 30 verso-31 recto.
51   Adam von Bremen 1917, p. 265 (IV. xxxii).
52   Saxo 1 1979, p. 153.
53   Zieglerus-Krantzius 1583, p. 482. On him: Günther and Lauchert 1900, p. 176-177.
54   Münster 1550 (1968), p. 987.
55   Zieglerus-Krantzius 1583, p. 483 484.

They were certainly not stupid. But their speech was crude, more like a grinding of teeth, understandable to no one, not even their neighboring tribes. It was for this reason and no other that they conducted their trade by leaving hides at a designated spot and returning later to see what had been given in return.[56] This also explains why they were called Lapps, fools or innocents—Finn-Lapps, of course, as they were labeled on the maps to distinguish them from the Wild Lapps who lived up in the mountains, an even shyer tribe of faun-like men and bearded women who seldom allowed themselves to be captured.[57] Some authorities claimed that even farther to the north there were Pygmies, creatures no taller than ten-year-old children, who uttered only a kind of quacking sound and seemed more closely related to monkeys than to human beings.[58]

It was known for a fact that the people who lived farther along the coast, past the White Sea, were the same as these Skrittfinns or Finn-Lapps or Samoyeds. That was in Biarmaland, a region inhabited by giants, according to the older medieval writers—a sort of borderland between the natural and the supernatural world, where human heads mounted on stakes and gigantic dogs frightened off all intruders. Saxo maintained that the Samoyeds living there were as adept at sorcery as the Finns. They could change the weather at will, call downpours, thunder, and lightning down upon their enemies, or suddenly surprise them with a sweltering heat even more terrible than the worst cold.[59] They seemed, in any case, almost identical to the Finn-Lapps of Kola with their sleighs, curved slats, and tents made of animal skins.

These Samoyeds, or Iuhri if you will, must in turn have been the same as the Lucomories described by Von Herberstein. So many names. In winter no one saw them; they withdrew so far into their forests and caves that they seemed to die out completely. But when the sun returned and the snow began to melt on the southern slopes and along the river banks, they would reappear. Twice a year they came together at a designated spot near the Pechora River to exchange their goods with the Russians and Tartars.[60]

Richard Johnson, who accompanied his master Richard Chancellor on the voyage past Novaya Zemlya in 1556, paid a visit to this tribe and described the experience in his report. He commented that the Samoyeds living on the island of Vaygach, between Novaya Zemlya and the Russian coast, were particularly dangerous. They killed every Russian who set foot on land there, and ate them up. But even more dangerous, he maintained, were the Samoyeds at the mouth of the Ob'; given the chance, they would murder anyone who did not speak their language.[61]

Johnson was present at one of their magic seances on January 5, 1556. No one from western Europe had ever experienced anything like it, and his description is vivid with detail:

---

56   Zieglerus-Krantzius 1583, p. 484; Adam von Bremen 1917, p. 266 (IV. xxxii).

57   Adam von Bremen 1917, p. 266 (IV. xxxii); see also the map of Claudius Clavus in Nordenskiöld 1889 (1970), p. 49, ill. 27.

58   Jovius-Grynaeus 1532, p. 472.

59   Saxo 1 1979, p. 263-265 and 286.

60   Hakluyt 1, 1598, p. 284.

61   Hakluyt 1 1598, p. 281.

Every kindred doth sacrifice in their own tent, and he that is most ancient is their priest. And first the priest doth begin to play upon a thing like a great sieve, with a skin on the one end like a drum: and the stick that he playeth with is about a span long and one end is round like a ball, covered with the skin of a hart. Also the priest hath on his head a thing of white like a garland, and his face is covered with a piece of shirt of mail, with many small ribs and teeth of fishes and wild beasts hanging on the same mail.

Then he singeth as we use here in England to hallo, whoop or shout at hounds, and the rest of the company answer him with the chant "Igha, Igha, Igha," and then the priest replieth again with his voice. And they answer him with the selfsame words so many times that in the end he becometh as it were mad, falling down as he were dead, having nothing on him but a shirt, lying upon his back. And I might perceive him to breathe.

I asked them why he lay so, and they answered me, "Now doth our God tell him what we shall do, and whither we shall go."

And when he had lain still a little while, they cried thus three times together, "Oghao, Oghao, Oghao," and as they use these three calls he riseth with his head and lieth down again. And then he rose up and sang with like voice as he did before, and his audience answered him, "Igha, Igha, Igha." Then he commanded them to kill five elk or great deer, and continued singing still, both he and they, as before. Then he took a sword of a cubit and a span long (I did mete it myself) and put it into his belly halfway and sometime less, but no wound was to be seen (they continuing in their sweet song still). Then he put the sword into the fire till it was warm, and so thrust it into the slit of his shirt and thrust it through his body, as I thought, in at his navel and out at his fundament. The point being out of his shirt behind, I laid my finger upon it. Then he pulled out the sword and sat down.

This being done, they set a kettle of water over a fire to heat, and when the water doth seethe, the priest beginneth to sing again, they answering him. For so long as the water was in heating they sat and sang not. Then they made a thing being four-square and in height and squareness of a chair, and covered with a gown very close the forepart thereof, for the hinder part stood to the tent's side… The water still seething on the fire, and this square seat being ready, the priest put off his shirt and the thing like a garland which was on his head with those things which covered his face, but he had on yet all this while a pair of hose of deer skins with hair on which came up to his buttocks. So he went into the square seat and sat down like a tailor and sang with a strong voice…

Then they took a small line made of deer's skins of four fathoms long, and with a final knot the priest made it fast about his neck and under his left arm and gave it unto two men standing on both sides of him, which held the ends together. Then the kettle of hot water was set before him in the square seat. All this time the square seat was not covered, and then it was covered in a gown or broad cloth without lining, such as the Russians do wear. The two men which did hold the ends of the line, still standing there, began to draw, and drew till they had drawn the ends of the line stiff and together. And then I heard a thing fall into the kettle of water which was before him in the tent.

Thereupon I asked them that sat by me what it was that fell into the water that stood before him. And they answered me that it was his head, his shoulder and his left arm, which the line hath cut off... Then I rose up and would have looked whether it were so or not, but they laid hold on me and said that if they should see him with their bodily eyes they should live no longer. And the most part of them can speak the Russian tongue to be understood; and they took me to be a Russian. Then they began to hallo with these words, "Oghaoo, Oghaoo, Oghaoo," many times together. And as they were thus singing and outcalling, I saw a thing like a finger of a man two times together thrust through the gown of the priest. I asked them that sat next to me what it was that I saw, and they said not his finger, for he was yet dead, and that which I saw appear through the gown was a beast, but what beast they knew not nor would not tell. And I looked upon the gown and there was no hole to be seen. And then at the last the priest lifted up his head with his shoulder and arm and all his body, and came forth to the fire.

Thus far of their service which I saw during the space of certain hours... And I went to him that served the priest and asked what their god said to him when he lay as dead. He answered that his own people doth not know, neither is it for them to know; for they must do as he commanded. [62]

Such a tribe they were: uncivilized, wild and hostile. But too intimidating to visit? No, certainly not. For that the hides they offered to trade were much too valuable on western markets. So Brunel bought and traded. In Lampas, the meeting place east of Kholmogory,[63] he exchanged his stock of bells and mirrors for sable and ermine.[64] He may also have collected for the tsar of all Russians, or for the Stroganovs as representatives of the tsar, the hides which the Samoyeds owed him in tribute since they had been subjugated.[65] And while he tied the dirty hides into bundles, loaded them onto his sleighs in leather sacks reeking of walrus oil, and later transferred them to his ship, he kept observing, kept asking questions.

That was not far from where the island Vaygach obstructed the passage between Novaya Zemlya and the mainland. The narrow channel which Burrough had managed to find was usually unnavigable because of ice floes. But at times the current could almost magically cause the ice to vanish overnight, the mist would rise, and open water would appear ahead. It had to be possible to reach the mouth of the Ob' by this route. There were, after all, Russians who managed it in their lodyas.[66] And once at the mouth of the Ob' they would have clear sailing over inland waterways—up the Ob' and the Ardoh to the Lake of Kittay, or whatever other names they were known by.

From Lampas he went to Kola and from Kola, together with Grigory, Yakov, Semyon or another member of the Stroganov family, to Dordrecht. They probably traveled in a ship from Antwerp or Enkuizen or some other Netherlandic port. For the first time in years Brunel spoke Dutch again. And for the first time, too, he heard of all the

---

62   Hakluyt 1 1598, p. 284-285.
63   Hakluyt 1 1598, p. 284.
64   Massa-Gerritsz 1924, p. 13.
65   Michov-Grynaeus 1532, p. 446.
66   Hakluyt 1 1598, p. 280.

unrest—almost a revolution—taking place in his native country. However, Brunel was carrying proof of good business opportunities. He had already managed to establish contacts for longer-term cooperation in Dordrecht, and they would yield even better results if he could interest one of the leading merchants of Antwerp, Gillis Hooftman for example, in his trading ventures in Kola.

But the dream of Cathay must have kept shimmering through all these activities. It was not only the desire for wealth. It was also, in the mud and cold of the north and in prosperous Antwerp as well, a dream of a culture unlike any other in the world. Of bathhouses and palaces, parks and pleasure boats with silken cushions. Of a kingdom where one could, above all, travel from the south to the far north without fear of war or robbers, and at the end of each day find an inn with comforts fit for a prince. The stories lived on—as an inkling of what life could be like.

IV *Antwerp*

In the years Olivier Brunel spent wandering through Russia, from Kazan' to Astrakhan and through the land of the Tartars beyond the Urals, Antwerp had become a bustling center of commercial, political, and scientific activity. The city now numbered ninety thousand inhabitants, ten to fifteen thousand of whom had turned their backs on the mother church to become Mennonites, Lutherans, and Calvinists.[1]

The Calvinists were the most vehement group. In the late summer of 1566 they had destroyed images in one church after another, and in March of the following year they tried to seize power in Antwerp. At first they put pressure on the leading Lutheran merchant, Gillis Hooftman (see ill. 21), as well as others of his conviction, to join their side. But when these people showed no sympathy for such adventures, they began to plot the expulsion of both Lutherans and Catholics from the city. They did not succeed. The result, however, was that the city was placed under the direct rule of the new governor, the Duke of Alva.[2]

Peace had been restored, it seemed. Many Calvinists fled the country and their leaders were summoned to appear before the Council of Blood, twenty-five men from Antwerp alone. But there was no general persecution of Protestants, except for the revolutionary-minded Mennonites. Certainly Lutherans were allowed to live in peace. The incursions across the southern and northern borders in 1568 by the Prince of Orange, who had earlier fled the country, were no more than minor provocations. A general amnesty was declared in 1570 and soon after that the first refugees began returning.[3] Everything was going to be all right.

Hooftman's business was flourishing. As a Lutheran he had little to fear after 1566, despite the claims of Spanish spies that he was secretly a Calvinist. That was nonsense, although he did have his contacts.[4] At least a hundred ships of his were sailing the seas from North Africa to Danzig. As one of the most important figures in the trade with England and France, he imported wood from Russia, textiles from England, pastel and wine from Toulouse.[5] He, if anyone, was an example of how far an energetic and intelligent man could go. The poor young man of twenty who had arrived in Antwerp with no means of support had managed, through hard work, to become one of the richest

---

1   Thijs 1990, p. 10-13.
2   Groenveld-Leeuwenberg 1979, p. 74-75; Haecht 1 1929, p. 194-197; Prims 8.1 1941, p. 102-105; Marnef 1996, p. 101-105.
3   Groenveld-Leeuwenberg 1979, p. 84-85; Prims 8.1 1941, p. 107-108.
4   Thijs 1990, p. 22; Zweite 1980, p. 71-72; Marnef 1996, p. 150.
5   Berens 1968, p. 67 and 74; Brulez 1959, p. 16 and 452-453; Wee 2 1963, p. 226; Coornaert 1 1961, p. 345, 2 1961, p. 42 and 77; Smet 1 1950, p. 295-297.

21.   *The Antwerp Merchant Gillis Hooftman and his Wife.*
      By Maarten de Vos (1570).

citizens of the town, with a house near the fortress, the "Castle," and large warehouses on the nearby Wharf.[6] Always busy, he poured his energy into making new contacts, opening up possibilities, taking the wind out of the sails of the English sea trade.[7]

His nautical knowledge surpassed that of all the other merchants. He collected sea charts and instruments for calculating sailing directions in order to reduce to a minimum the risks of being driven off course or, worse, of being shipwrecked. But he also bought geographical maps wherever he could find them—not only to calculate distances, loading weights and the best routes, but also to assess the reports of wars raging in various places. When his pupil and later son-in-law Johan Radermacher came up with the idea of collecting small-format maps which could be bound together as a book, he was immediately interested.[8]

---

6   Berens 1968, p. 74-77; Brulez 1959, p. 22 and 223; Denucé (1938), p. 15; Prims 8.2 1942, p. 260.
7   Smet 1 1950, p. 295-297.
8   Meskens 1994, p. 126.

22. *Abraham Ortelius.*
    By Philips Galle.

The project was placed in the hands of the Antwerp map merchant Abraham Ortelius (see ill. 22). That was around 1554. In the years which followed, Ortelius managed, through his travels and correspondence, to collect thirty-eight maps. They were to become not only the pride of the Hooftman company, but also the core of the atlas comprising fifty-two maps which Ortelius placed on the market in 1572, the *Theatrum Orbis Terrarum*.[9]

One of the men with whom Ortelius immediately made contact upon receiving his commission was Gerard Mercator, the famous geographer who a short time earlier had entered the service of the Duke of Clève and settled in Duisburg.[10] While Ortelius was building up his collection, Mercator worked on his world map which eventually appeared in 1569—a map designed to help seamen plot their course and prevent them from becoming hopelessly lost. The main problem was how to project the globe onto a flat surface, and until then no one had found a truly satisfactory solution. Now that long-distance voyages to unknown regions were becoming the order of the day the problem was even more pressing. Mercator suggested that the degrees of latitude could be gradually enlarged towards the poles to keep them proportional to the degrees of longitude— this also meant that the location of places relative to one another would not be distorted.[11]

At the same time he developed a separate projection for the polar region with the pole itself at the center, and printed it in the lower left-hand corner of the large world map. Voyages through the northern waters were, after all, the latest thing since the foundation of the Muscovy Company. Mercator corresponded with John Dee, the geographer who, together with Sebastian Cabot, was one of the earliest advisors of the English company.[12] Dee, whom he knew from his time in Louvain, supplied him with information which Burrough and Chancellor, and later Jenkinson as well, had brought

9   Ortelius 1887, nr. 330, p. 772-773, 776-778 and nr. 331, p. 787 and 790-791; Meurer 1991, p. 26-28; Karrow 1993, p. 4-5.
10 Ortelius 1887, nr. 331, p. 791; Houtte 1963, p. 7-8; Tromnau 1994, p. 11-13.
11 Keuning 1946, p. 86-87; Karrow 1993, p. 389; Kretschmer 1995, p. 68-75.
12 French 1984, p. 178-179.

back regarding the northern coast of Russia and the location of Moscow.[13] Ortelius also kept in contact with Dee after the English scholar's visit to Antwerp in 1563-64, and it was probably through him that he managed to acquire the map which Jenkinson had made of Russia.[14]

Hooftman—who had his own representative in London since Johan Radermacher had settled there in 1567[15]—must have kept a close eye on all these developments, waiting for the right moment to send one of his own ships past North Cape. Uncertain adventures to Cathay or anywhere else were not for him. As a good merchant he knew the risks. But neither did he like to let opportunities pass him by. That was the art: being prepared, recognizing possibilities when they presented themselves, knowing where to find the reports that were available and knowing how to assess them, sending a young man up north to learn Russian, to look around…

CHRISTOPHORVS PLANTINVS,
TVRONENSIS.

Qui Plantine bonas hoc tempore iußerat artes
Crefcere, te iußit præla parare Deus.
Omnia χϱύσα, inquit, doctorum fcripta manebunt,
Hæc pius excudat dummodo Chriſtophorus.
E 4

23.   *Christoffel Plantijn.*
      By Philips Galle (1572).

But there were more reasons for immersing one's self in the science of geography. John Dee, for example, was primarily interested in the deep wisdom and occult knowledge of the East, although he certainly did not spurn material gain.[16] For Mercator, too, cartographic and geographic research was part of a much broader plan to describe the origin and nature of the earth in order to arrive at True Wisdom. Whatever that might be. The paths of the stars as well as the course of human history—its array of empires, the genealogies of noble families starting with the creation of the world and the migrations of peoples—all had a bearing on his work.[17]

This kind of geographical and historical speculation flourished in Antwerp, especially since the great printer Christoffel Plantijn (see ill. 23) had started preparing what he considered the publication of his lifetime, the eight thick volumes of the multilingual royal Bible, the *Biblia Regia*, or *Polyglot*, as it was commonly called. After giving his royal approval to the plans, Philip II appointed the Spanish cleric Benito Arias Montano to supervise the project (see ill. 24). Plantijn had his misgivings, but the arrangement turned out to work surprisingly well. Soon after Montano's arrival in 1568 the

---

13   Skelton 1962, p. 159-160; Taylor 1968, p. 78 and p. 85-87; Dreyer-Eimbcke 1994, p. 148-155.
14   Ortelius 1570 (1964), leaf 46 "Russia"; Taylor 1968, p. 87-88 and 98-99; Dorsten 1973, p. 22; French 1984, p. 5; Schilder 2 1987, p. 48; Karrow 1993, p. 318-320.
15   Heezen-Stoll 1990, p. 674.
16   French 1984, p. 181; see also Ortelius 1887, nr. 67, letter by Dee to Ortelius, p. 159.
17   Geske 1962, p. 259-260; Thiele 1994, p. 17-18; Van der Krogt 1994, p. 103.

two became fast friends, and the newcomer was drawn into the circle of scholars who made Plantijn's publishing house a center of European culture. Nowhere, he wrote in his letters back home, was there such vibrant intellectual activity, so much scholarly and scientific enthusiasm, such fruitful cooperation.[18]

Montano's own contribution to the *Polyglot* consisted mainly of the 'Apparatus,' a treatise on Jewish antiquities which filled a large part of the eighth volume. It included chapters on clothing and measurements, on the ark of the covenant and the temple, on the oldest language, and on the dispersion of peoples over the earth (see ill. 25).[19]

This historical geography was based largely on tradition. Jewish and Christian writers of late antiquity had already speculated about the repopulation of the earth after the flood. Shem, Ham and Japheth, the three sons of Noah, had each been allotted a region: Japheth received Europe, Shem Asia, and Ham Africa. Their sons, in turn, became the progenitors of the various peoples of the world. All through the Middle Ages scholars had made efforts to identify them with ethnic groups mentioned by Pliny

24. *Benito Arias Montano.*
By Jan Wierickx.

and other classical writers, as well as with those known during their own time.[20] As early as 600 A.D. Isidore of Seville traced the line of Japheth's second son Magog through the Scythian tribe of Massagetae, or Getae, mentioned by Pliny, to the Goths. Similarly Gomer, the oldest son, came to be associated with the Cimbri, and his son Aschenaz with the Germans. And Muscovites were said to have descended from Japheth's son Mesech or Mosech.[21]

Montano maintained that Ripath, another son of Gomer, had gone even farther north than Magog and Mesech into the region of the Ripaean Mountains, a land so remote that nothing was known of its borders. He believed that descendants of Ripath were still living there. More sensational, however, was what he reported about Shem's two descendants, Seba and Ophir. They had migrated eastward, Ophir even farther than Seba. He had traveled along the coast of the great sea in northern Russia and penetrated deep into the new world recently rediscovered by Columbus and Vespucci. There the two syllables of his name, Ophir, or Opire, had been reversed into Peru. This was the land which King Solomon had visited so long ago and where gold could still be found in abundance.[22]

---

18   Rekers 1961, p. 23-24.
19   Rekers 1961, p. 110.
20   Cf. Borst 1 1957, 2.1. 1958, 2.2. 1959, 3.1 1960, passim.
21   Borst 2.1 1958, p. 446, 2.2 1959, p. 1065 and 3.1, 1960, p. 1129.
22   Montanus 1593, p. 16-17 and p. 20.

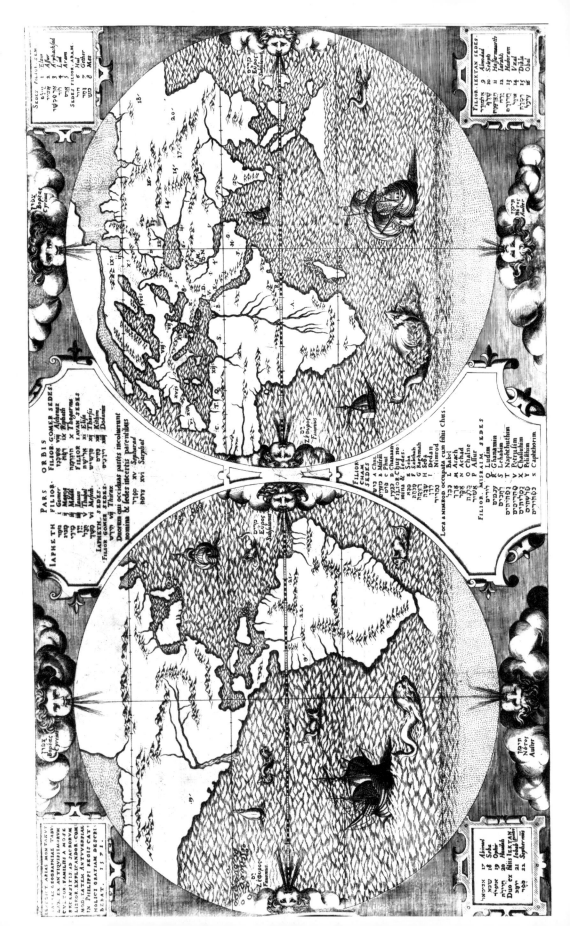

25. (Illustration page 70.)
    Benito Arias Montano, *The Dispersion of Peoples over the Earth.*
    The sons of Japheth were believed to be the ancestors of the European peoples: Magog (II) of the Goths, Gomer (I) of the Cimbri and his son Ashkenaz (VIII) of the Germans, and Meshech (VI) of the Muscovites. Gomer's son Riphath (IX) ended up even farther north. And Shem's descendants Sheba (18) and Ophir (19) were said to have migrated to the east. Ophir, it was believed, gave his name to Peru.

The map accompanying Montano's treatise made it all very clear: between Asia and America was a broad strip of land which continued above North America, forming a single land mass with the arctic continent. Neither a northeast nor a northwest passage was possible.[23] For did not the gold of South America and the etymology of the name Peru prove the existence of a land connection and therefore rule out anything like a Strait of the Three Brothers, or the Anian Strait, as it seemed to be called nowadays?

So far so good. But according to his physician friend Joannes Goropius, also known as Becanus (see ill. 26), Montano did not go far enough:

- "You shouldn't believe everything the classical authors say. They wrote such nonsense, and not only because they lacked the necessary scientific knowledge."
- "Aren't you exaggerating a little?"
- "Exaggerating? That it's supposed to be warmer at the north pole than anywhere else? Or that the moon is so much closer there that you can see the hills on his surface?[24]
- "His?"
- "In Cimbrian moon is a masculine noun. Seriously, the fables and poems of the ancients contain a lot of hidden truth, no doubt, but you have to know geography and languages other than Greek and Latin if you want to get to the bottom of it all."[25]

26. *Joannes Goropius Becanus.*

23 Montanus 1593, p. 26-27.
24 Becanus 1569, p. 1015-1017.
25 Becanus 1569, p. 992, 994 and 1048.

They often talked about these matters, in the garden of Plantijn's house on the Friday Market and later at Montano's bedside after the northern climate proved too much for him in the winter of 1569. For a friend, Becanus was still prepared to put his medical knowledge to use, though he hardly practiced his profession any longer, immersed as he was in his historical studies.[26]

Montano probably considered Becanus' interpretations too far-fetched for such a monumental work as the *Biblia Regia*, which also needed the approval of the Vatican censors. His book would have to be published independently, especially since it focused more on the history of Antwerp than on that of the Bible. Becanus could insist all he liked that his intention was to demonstrate the truth of the one Catholic faith by showing the harmony between ancient history, classical poetry and Holy Scripture, his friend would do no more than write a recommendation for a royal gratuity. Becanus himself could then phrase a dedication to Philip II in a way which placed the work in the context of the Biblical edition.[27]

It was definitely a strange book. Plantijn, who published it, told of various scholars who were amazed to find it much more solidly researched than they had first thought.[28] He himself felt a deep admiration for Becanus, who had, after all, given him financial help in setting up his business with the annuity he received as the former personal physician of Charles V's two sisters.[29]

Becanus of course also believed Japheth to be the forefather of the European peoples, and his son Gomer the ancestor of the Cimbri. But his ideas about the tribes which classical authors like Pliny had situated in the far north—the Scythians, Issedonians, Arimaspi and Hyperboreans—were quite different from those current in his day. In his opinion, the ancient Greeks had situated the Hyperboreans with their happy life and mild climate at the pole only because they thought there was no more land above the extreme northern part of Europe. They had no idea that there were also people living beyond the pole, in the other hemisphere.

In later centuries, too, it was always believed that land on the other side of the earth started only at the equator, the Atlantis of Plato which was said to extend all the way down to the south pole. People in modern times had crossed the ocean directly to South America for just this reason. Great quantities of gold had been found there—so much that not only Spain but all of Europe had been corrupted by it—but no Hyperboreans because they lived up in the northern hemisphere.[30]

The homelands of the various peoples and tribes could be deduced from their names. However—and when he came to this point some bitterness would tinge the voice of the learned physician—a person really had to know Cimbrian, in other words German, or what was then called "Diets." For it was sheer nonsense to think that the tribes would give themselves names in any language but their own, and they were all Cimbri, even the Hyperboreans, that much was sure.[31]

---

26 Rekers 1961, p. 24, 146-147 and 275.
27 Becanus 1569, p. b 2 recto-verso; Rekers 1961, p. 147.
28 Voet 2 1972, p. 293.
29 Voet 1 1968, p. 368-369; Voet 2 1972, p. 469; Brouwer 1953, p. 272; Bostoen 1991, p. 157-158.
30 Becanus 1569, p. 1017-1018, 1032-1034.
31 Becanus 1569, p. 1011-1013.

First came the Scythians. Their territory stretched over the entire breadth of Europe and Asia, as far as Cathay. Their neighbors, the Issedonians, lived along the Arctic Sea. That was obvious, since "is" was "ice," "se" was "sea" and "don" meant "nearby." All the tribes along the northern coasts, whether they were Lapps or Samoyeds, Iuhri or one of the others, were Issedonians. And beyond the Issedonians lived the Arimaspi. Herodotus had maintained that their name meant "one-eyed people," but that was nonsense which he had heard from some Scythian, no doubt, and which he had been gullible enough to believe since his knowledge of Cimbrian was nil. "Har" meant "burning cold," "rim" was "rime" or "frost," "hast" was "hasty" and "spu" meant "spout." Put them together and you get "sudden-torrent-of-burning-cold." So that must have referred to the region of the coldest and most penetrating winds in the extreme northeast, near Anian. They were called "one-eyed" because they wrapped themselves from head to foot in animal skins, leaving only a small opening for their face. "Eye," after all, could also mean "hole," as in the expression "the eye of the needle." This also explained the stories about Cyclopes, like the one found in the report of the Frisian noblemen.

The list of tribes which one would encounter made it clear that in antiquity the route to the Hyperboreans crossed the north of Asia. There was no alternative, for the Arctic Sea blocked what would have been a shorter route via the pole. If the Muscovites and Tartars who presently inhabited these areas could be induced to make peace and allow free passage, it would still be the best route.

- "To Cathay and Kinsai?"
- "To Cathay and Kinsai, but also to the northern half of the American continent, the part attached by only a narrow isthmus to the southern half—the area we know so little about."
- "Bacalaos."
- "Or Estotiland, or whatever else they call it."

But now, too, the thought of the griffins frightened people away. Not birds of prey anymore, half-eagle and half-lion, but rapacious human beings whom the Arimaspi called "grypes," a name derived from the verb "to grasp," or "to grab." Pliny had also believed that the original griffin had existed only in legends, on this one point the doctor agreed with him. In Paris he had once seen a claw which could have belonged to such a creature, a curiosity as fascinating as the gigantic pitch-black horn owned by his former patient, the Queen of Hungary, sister of Charles V. In his opinion, however, these were forgeries, like the unicorn horn which fishermen had brought from the seas near Lapland and which was still on view here in Antwerp. The spongy piece of bone which would have attached it to the forehead was in itself proof that the horn could not have belonged to a four-legged beast.[32] More likely it was the tusk of a fish like the ones pictured on Olaus Magnus' sea chart, horrible monsters with the horns and tusks of wild animals.[33]

---

32   Becanus 1569, p. 1032 and 1035-1038.
33   Nordenskiöld 1889 (1970), p. 59, ill. 32.

But to return to the griffins: the story of a bird which carried living horses and cows off into the sky could have originated in Norway, where one type of eagle seems to have preyed on calves and hares. Stories of this kind always grew in the telling. But the underlying truth was that the Arimaspi described their neighbors as thieves and plunderers. Like all Cimbrian peoples, they loved fables and fantasies. The entire story of the bird could be explained by the fact that beyond the Arimaspi lived a people who wore cloaks and headdresses made of bird feathers. That much had become clear since the discovery of the new world, where the natives still wore such things.

Becanus himself owned a headdress of this kind which he enjoyed showing to his visitors. Although it had come from Brazil and not from the northern region, there was no reason to assume that the people there did not have them as well. In any case, the comparison with birds could be explained not only from their feathers but also from their swiftness. They could run faster than any other people on earth, and any stranger who dared to set foot on their territory they seized and devoured. It was because of this lion-like habit that the Arimaspi had described them as having the body of a lion. Later writers attributed this cannibalism to the easternmost Scythians because they could not imagine that there were any tribes beyond them. The doctor, however, insisted that the Arimaspi had made up the story to frighten all other peoples away from the American gold.

That was how the tale of griffins guarding unimaginable hoards of gold in the north had come about. The precious stones were later additions, as were the horses and cows which they carried off—an impossible feat because wings capable of lifting such weight would be too heavy to fly. That much was proved by the ostrich, the strongest bird on earth, which never left the ground.

All this showed, in short, that the territory of the Cimbrian tribes extended as far as Plato's Atlantis, now called Brazil. The extreme north of Europe's hemisphere was inhabited by Arimaspi, and Hyperboreans was the name which they gave to everyone living beyond them, in other words across the pole in the other hemisphere, as far down as the tropic of Cancer and the equator. To everyone, that is, living beyond the region dominated by Boreas, the northeast-by-east wind. The Arimaspi gave them names in their own language, of course, "past-extreme-north-northeast" or something of that sort. But the Greeks, who found that too difficult to pronounce and who did not even have such a complex system for distinguishing thirty-two different wind directions, had probably abbreviated the name in Greek.

The Hyperborean Mountains were found there as well, and extended all the way down to Florida. They were also called the Ripaean Mountains, from "rhi," meaning "horse-riding," and "pai," meaning "pacify" or "placate." In any case they were not in Scandinavia, as Arias Montano also believed, for the mountains there were not at all accessible on horseback. Moreover northern Scandinavia was an impossible habitat for the happiest of all the Cimbrian tribes, as Pliny had described the Hyperboreans.[34] There was probably nothing more to be discovered up there than the Arctic Sea. But even if there were more land—Greenland, for instance, said to be so rich in butter—and even if that Greenland were not an island but part of a continent which extended as far as the pole, the nights would still be too long there, and the cold too intense.

---

34   Pliny 2 1969, p. 186-189 (IV. xii. 88-91).

- "If I were younger I'd go up there myself and do some investigating."
- "Investigating what?"
- "Everything. The truth about the griffins, the location of Greenland, the homeland of the Hyperboreans."
- "Oh, right. You'd take a ship into the icy cold and live for weeks on sea biscuit and spoiled slop with at most a swig of brandy now and then to keep the damp out of your joints."
- "Or overland."

For the road to the Hyperboreans ran from the Donau through the north of Russia and Asia and on into North America, on that point the learned doctor agreed with his learned patient. Long before the time of Solomon, people had traveled there for the gold, either across the great ocean or along this land route.[35] Might it really be possible then?

So it was, that while an Antwerp merchant like Gillis Hooftman pored over reports of seamen and commercial agents, scholars in that same city were moving entire peoples across the face of Europe and Asia, and even to the farthest corners of newly discovered America. All available knowledge, not only from antiquity but also that of church fathers, medieval scholars and the Arabs, was brought to bear on the great riddle of creation. How exactly? And when? And, especially, for what purpose?

There was no shortage of documentation. The large publishing houses had seized the opportunity offered by printing to compile huge quantities of information. Not just one chronicle followed by one or two more, which could then be meticulously compared and harmonized. That was how it used to be done. Now everything had to be printed, and every text as an integral edition. Readers could then make their own comparisons.

As early as 1493, immediately after Columbus' first discoveries became known, Peter Martyr in Spain began recording information about the new lands. His work, *On the New World*, appeared serially between 1511 and 1530. In the end, including all the additions published until his death in 1526, it comprised eight volumes of ten chapters each.[36] Meanwhile Symon Grynaeus began collecting reports about peoples in the north and east who for the most part had not been mentioned by classical authors. His compilation included the books by the Armenian Haithon and the Cracow canon Mathias of Michov about the Tartars, as well as Paulus Jovius' adaptation of the work by the Russian emissary Demetrius on all the lands ruled by the tsar. It first appeared in 1532, both in Basel and Paris, and was soon reprinted.[37] But the crowning work was the collection by the Italian Battista Ramusio which appeared in three weighty volumes between 1563 and 1574 and which included virtually all the information about journeys and tribes found in the writings of Marco Polo and other medieval travelers. This work was also reprinted, one of the volumes even a third time.[38] Meanwhile, in England, Richard Hakluyt was working on a compilation based largely—although, according to reports, certainly not exclusively—on journeys by Englishmen.[39]

---

35 Becanus 1569, p. 1038-1042 and 1046-1047.
36 Martyr 1 1972, p. 5-8.
37 Grynaeus 1532; *Nouvelle biographie générale* 22 1858, p. 272-273.
38 Ramusio 1 1978, p. xxiv-xxv and xxxvii.
39 Laughton 1890, p. 11-12.

The northern regions formed the special focus of a book by Albert Krantz of Hamburg, which brought together information found in Saxo, Giraldus, Adam of Bremen and other older writers. It finally appeared in 1546, thirty years after Krantz's death, when that part of the world was finally starting to attract interest. Later editions also included Jacob Ziegler's book on Scandinavia.[40] But all these writings would soon be considered outdated upon the publication in 1555 of the standard work by the Swedish bishop Olaus Magnus. As early as 1539 he had published a map showing all of Scandinavia, including a part of Biarmaland, Iceland and a small tip of Greenland. The map was illustrated with pygmies, Lapps in sleighs and on skis, ferocious animals, a griffin, and sea monsters of all sorts.[41] Now, in exile in Rome, he had come out with his book, a splendid folio volume printed on heavy paper and richly illustrated. Between its covers was all the knowledge, but also all the nonsense, of earlier centuries. Plantijn published a smaller format of this work in 1558, leaving out all the extraneous and erroneous material; and this edition was soon reprinted as well.[42]

So there was no shortage of factual information. The shelves and cupboards of Antwerp book dealers could hardly contain it all. Expensive as they were, these books were in demand, especially by scholars. At least scholars like Becanus who had a few florins to spare. Montanus sent large chests full of books to his patrons in Spain.[43]

It all seemed so urgent. Times were strange, full of dark forebodings as never before. Entire peoples were rising up against their lawful rulers. Families were torn apart by religious strife, sons against fathers, brothers against brothers, wives against their husbands. Women appeared to be taking control of things, and the entire world seemed topsy-turvy. No wonder many people believed that the coming of the Antichrist was imminent. If it did not happen in 1556 as predicted, then it would certainly happen in 1566 or soon thereafter. This event would herald the return of the Messiah and the beginning of the thousand-year reign of God on earth. But how much blood and how many tears would be shed before that moment arrived…[44]

One thing was certain: the history of the world and the dispersion of its peoples over the earth were part of an all-embracing divine plan which would culminate in the definitive triumph of Christendom.

Christoffel Plantijn probably owed the idea for his five-language eight-volume Bible to Guillaume Postel, whom he had visited in Paris in 1563 (see ill. 27).[45] Since then, this blustering scholar, with his eccentric and even heretical ideas about universal Christianity and the times preceding the second coming of Christ, had been imprisoned by the French government in the monastery of Saint Martin des Champs. He was clearly considered insane—fortunately perhaps, for he had already spent four years in the prisons of the Inquistion in Rome and owed his freedom only to the riots which had broken out after the death of Pope Paul IV.

---

40   Thoroddsen 1 1897, p. 120-123; Grobecker 1979, col. 673-674.
41   Knauer 1981, p. 7-10.
42   Magnus 1555; Magnus 1558, cf. also p. 2 a verso; Magnus 1562.
43   Rekers 1961, p. 23-24.
44   Bouwsma 1957, p. 273 and 281; Kunz 1981, p. 144-147.
45   Rekers 1961, p. 97-98; Kunz 1981, p. 162-163.

27. *Guillaume Postel.*
By Jean Rabel.

All the same, there was no one in the western world so well-versed in Arabic, Syriac and Chaldean. Behind the scenes he made a sizable contribution to Plantijn's Bible, although this was kept as quiet as possible to avoid jeopardizing the project.[46]

The intention behind the *Polyglot* was to present Christianity to peoples who had no more than vague notions about it, especially Jews and Turks. On this point everyone was in agreement, including the Spanish king who had agreed to finance the project.[47] For Postel, however, that was only one step in a much larger plan which he set forth in a steady stream of publications. The goal, as he saw it, was to restore the original unity of the world under one king, one law and one faith which would be confirmed by the return of Christ. Only then would it be possible to drive out the Antichrist, only then could the thousand-year reign begin. To help bring this about it was necessary to know the origins of the peoples, to understand how they were related to and dependent on one another, and to fathom the forces of good and evil. Then, at last,

46   Bouwsma 1957, p. 24-26; Kunz 1981, p. 39-40, 116-117, 140, 162-165.
47   Rekers 1961, p. 98-100.

it would be possible to retrieve the principles of universal unity which Satan had thrown into confusion.[48]

On many points, of course, Postel's ideas differed very little from those of his scholarly contemporaries. On the matter of Japheth's sons, Gomer and Magog, and Gomer's son Ripath, who was said to have migrated to the far north, he agreed with Montano and Becanus—as he did on the question of Ophir migrating via Asia to Peru.[49] But his most important book on these topics, *Compendium of Cosmographical Knowledge Directed Towards its Final Aim, the Incontestable Proof for Divine Providence*, published in 1561 by Oporinus in Basel, contained some ideas all his own. Not only that Gomer, the oldest son of Japheth (himself Noah's oldest son) was the father of the Gauls and Umbrians as well as the Cimbri; also, according to primogeniture, world domination was the rightful heritage of the Gauls.[50]

The sheer absurdity of it all: the Germans, French and Italians originally a brotherhood of peoples, and first among them the French! Elsewhere Postel had stated in so many words that the French king was the person destined to destroy the Antichrist, whose seat of power was in the north.[51] Poor King Charles, only eleven years old. His mother, the regent, was only too willing to believe that this was all revolutionary rabble-rousing—and not of the harmless variety either, to judge from the size of the crowds attending Postel's lectures in Paris.[52]

- "If he would only keep out of politics."
- "Ridiculous, as if you can prove something on the basis of Hebrew. He doesn't even know Cimbrian. Sheer nonsense, all of it."
- "I'm not so sure. A lot of what he says about the Jewish diaspora, for instance, makes good sense to me. For centuries people have suspected that the ten lost tribes of Israel might be living somewhere in the far northeast of Asia."

According to Postel the two ethnic groups which had suddenly swept across Asia and into Europe three or four centuries earlier, the Tartars and the Turks, were originally Jews. He even believed the Tartars to be direct descendants of the ten lost tribes. In the northernmost corner of the world they fought against Gog and Magog of the tribe of Dan, oldest son of Rachel (by her handmaid Bilhah). This people, whom he called "Daniks," were the embodiment of evil, placed by Satan in the north and destined to bring forth the Antichrist.[53]

These last ideas Postel had not published, although he did correspond with Ortelius about them, and with others. One of his treatises, however, dealt with the Turks and the Tartars. Here he went to great lengths to prove that the Jewish tribes, which according to all reports lived walled in by mountains in an area called Arsareth, were the same as the Tartars. For were the latter not called—both by the Turks and by themselves—not

---

48   Bouwsma 1957, p. 129, 251-252, 272-275.
49   Postel 1561, p. 19-20, 24 and 32.
50   Postel 1561, p. 19-20, 22-25. Cf. also Postel 1969, p. 66-67 and Dubois 1972, p. 69-71.
51   Postel 1969, 184-187 and 203.
52   Bouwsma 1957, p. 26; Kunz 1981, p. 141-142.
53   Postel 1969, p. 163-164 and 182-184.

Tartars (as most Europeans referred to them), but Tatars or Totars? This in itself showed that they were related to the Turks. And was it not true that in Chaldean the word "totar" meant "accursed" and "lost?"

It was only with God's help that these Tartars suddenly emerged onto the world scene. Jewish prophecies foretold that they would unite with the other Jewish tribes and subsequently help establish the earthly kingdom of the Messiah. Time would tell how much of this was true. Postel was certain, in any case, that at a moment when they least expected it—and least deserved it—God's wisdom in the form of an angel had led them to elect a king, or khan, and to gather at the foot of a mountain on the coast of the Arctic Ocean. There they joined in prayer, beseeching God nine times for his forgiveness and begging him to set them free. At that moment the sea level lowered by nine feet, making it possible for people, animals and wagons to leave the area where they had been confined for so long.

They then moved across Europe, as far as Russia, Poland and Lithuania. Even the tsar of all Russians, though now a Greek Catholic, was originally a Tartar prince. They also migrated southeast, to Cathay and probably much farther yet, but their important move was to the west. For God had freed them in order to punish the pride of their brothers, the Turks, and to give support to the Christians. One of their khans even managed to take the caliph of Baghdad prisoner, and let him die of thirst and starvation in his own treasure chamber.[54]

In his *Compendium of Cosmographical Knowledge* published the following year, Postel added that while the lost Jewish tribes were still living in Arsareth, far to the north of China and Cathay, they had already been converted to Christianity by the Apostle Thomas. This, he maintained, was actually true of all the peoples of eastern Asia, including Japan. And since it was only a short distance between Japan and the northern part of the mysterious continent of Atlantis, now called America, it was not surprising that some knowledge of Christ and the cross had reached these regions as well. There were reports of a certain Quezalcouatlius who was known for his life of fasting and austerity, and who, in a white robe decorated with red crosses, taught the worship of a single God and preached that this earthly existence would be followed by eternal punishment and reward.

Later, however, the Jewish tribes lost the Holy Books through the wiles of Satan and internal strife. Knowledge of the gospel, and even the name of Christ, was forgotten, although there were still a few people among them who knew that their true name was Nazarenes.[55]

In Antwerp, in the high-ceilinged reading room of Plantijn's publishing house and with the sound of printing presses thudding in the background, Postel's book was read with excitement. There was Montano, sympathetic but cautious, as befitted a representative of the king; Plantijn himself, intrigued; and an outraged Becanus:

– "Totar," no less. And "Gheuth." Did you see this? The name "Goths" is supposed to come from the Hebrew "Gauth," or "Gheuth" as he spells it, because

---

54 Postel 1560, p. 23-27; Secret 1985, p. 302-303,
55 Postel 1561, p. 66-70.

the Goths are a jewel of the universe.[56] Goodness gracious. And this man is one of the team working on the *Biblia Regia*. If you ask me…"

The doctor's face flushed with anger. It had been bothering him for a long time, all those heretics and near heretics here in Antwerp, pretending all the while to be such good Catholics. Before long he left the city for good to settle in the prince bishopric of Liège.[57]

But just a short walk away, in his house The Lily on Old Lombard Street,[58] Ortelius was carefully penning information about the Totars and the ten tribes of Israel onto his map of Tartary (see ill. 28). He showed their original homeland, Arsareth, as extending into the Isthmus of Tabin, and noted that Gauthay, the name by which they were known in this region, indicated their special relationship with God. The word Cathay, he maintained, could also be traced back to this name—here one wonders whether he understood Postel correctly. Farther to the west he marked the mountain where they had gathered when God lowered the sea. North of this mountain lay the area where the Holy Books had been lost. More than a thousand miles farther, well beyond the seventieth degree of latitude, on an isthmus extending north, he situated the tribe of Naphtali, younger brother of Dan. They had settled there after the descendants of Dan, the Daniks or Denmarks, had been driven even farther north, to the region they now inhabited around the eightieth parallel—an area so frigid that no human being could ever travel through or around it.[59] Anyone intent on sailing to Cathay by the northeastern route had to be aware of this, Burrough and Chancellor most of all.

Most shocking, however, was what Postel had to say about the North Pole itself. It might have been wiser to say nothing on this subject, even though his ideas were founded on original Biblical and Cabalistic sources which had only recently been deciphered. For this went beyond ordinary historiography, straight to the heart of the Christian faith. And it was better to keep quiet about the faith ever since the Church, at the Council of Trent in the 1560's, had stated definitively what was true and what was not; since Philip II had given the Inquisition free rein; and since Antwerp had been placed under the direct rule of the Duke of Alva.[60]

The north was, of course, the seat of evil. But not in some vague and general way, nor in the purely figurative sense which Becanus had attached to it. The constellation Draco (Dragon), which wound around the pole, as well as Ursa Major and Ursa Minor, were not merely symbols of the devil and the fleshly lusts with which he tempted human beings, but signs of his actual presence.[61] The pole was literally the abode of Satan. God had chained him there for all eternity. This also explained all those demons and spirits in the region, all that shrieking and moaning. It was the black spot of the universe, the anchoring point of all matter from which evil emanated, and of gold, the root of all evil.

---

56   Postel 1561, p. 25.
57   De Brouwer 1953, p. 272.
58   Denucé 2 1913, p. 5.
59   Ortelius 1570, map 47 "Tartaria"; Secret 1985, p. 301-303. Cf. also Postel's letters to Ortelius of 1567 and 1579 in Ortelius 1887, nr. 10, p. 42-26 and nr. 81, p. 186-192; Schilder 2 1987, p. 63-65.
60   Prims 8.1 1941, p. 55-56 and 102-105.
61   Becanus 1569, p. 1053.

28. Abraham Ortelius, *Tartary* (1570).
    The regions inhabited by the ten tribes of Israel are shown in the east: Arsareth, their original home, is identified as the Isthmus of Tabin, and Tabor as the place where the Holy Books were lost; toward the north are the territories of the tribes of Naphtali and Dan.

Like a devastating storm, a cloud, a consuming fire, it would eventually engulf the world.

But because all evil was redeemed by the grace of God it was also the source of everything that was good. The evil came from Satan, there was no doubt about that. But the good sprang from nature as created by God, nature which in the north was so harsh and untamable that the people living there could hardly be anything but virtuous—with the help of Christ, of course. The north was therefore the gateway of both good and evil.[62]

He went even further, but only after hearing reports of Burroughs' discovery of Novaya Zemlya and his story that the highest mountain on earth was found there:[63] precisely because the north was the abode of Satan it also had to be the site of earthly Paradise. And all evidence pointed in that direction. Not only was the North Pole the most northern and therefore the highest point on earth, the place closest to heaven. There was also a mountain so high that its peak was continually in sunlight, even if at times no more than a single beam, like that of the rising sun, grazed its surface. Here, then, was absolute, fixed East—the eternal sunrise, "oriens"—and not in the Moluccan Islands or Cathay, where most theologians placed Paradise, because the eastern location of these places always depended on where one happened to be.

The Russians and other peoples in that region called the peak Sveta Gemla, holy mountain.[64] Here in the Hyperborean range, around this highest mountain on earth, raged the most violent storms. Desolate it was, and inaccessible, with its peak eternally covered with snow. But lower down in the valleys were fertile meadows with a wide range of flora and fauna. Here, where the sun shone for six months without setting, lived the happy Hyperboreans, or Ripaeans. After the great flood they had migrated as far north as possible, because no place was safer than where the attractive force of heaven was the strongest, drawing the earth upward to its greatest heights. They were the people with the longest life span and the greatest sense of justice in the world; they were also physically the strongest, the most capable of enduring hardship, the most patient and long-suffering…[65]

In the six years of Alva's rule, from 1567 to 1573, the cultural and scientific productivity of Antwerp reached an all-time peak. The eight volumes of the *Biblia Regia*, each numbering about seven hundred pages, appeared between 1569 and 1573.[66] Becanus' work on the origins of Antwerp, *Origines Antvverpianae*, was published in 1569, and Ortelius' *Theatrum* in 1570. The Dutch edition of this last work appeared the following year, translated by the schoolmaster Peter Heyns, whose pupils included Becanus' two young daughters.[67]

It still seemed possible that all the religious differences would disappear if people simply concentrated on inner communion with God and on imitating Christ in their everyday lives. Plantijn sometimes spoke forcefully on this subject in his circle of trusted friends:

---

62   Secret 1981, p. 36-37, 91-92; cf. Secret 1973, p. 88-89, 93 and 98.
63   Hakluyt 1 1598, p. 280.
64   Secret 1973, p. 100; Secret 1985, p. 305.
65   Postel 1561, p. 7-9, 24-25.
66   Rekers 1961, p. 109-110.
67   Ortelius 1571; Brouwer 1953, p. 272.

- "Let us obey the laws and commandments of God and of those who have been placed over us, without worrying about matters that do not concern us. Only with peace in our hearts and a tranquil mind can we serve the Lord, and that has nothing to do with doctrines and dogmas."

There were rumors that he was a follower of the House of Love, the sect led by the mysterious Hendrik Niclaes, or of his rival Hendrik Janszoon Barrefelt, otherwise known as Hiël.[68] But even a pious Catholic like Ortelius did not shy away from close contact with an equally pious Lutheran like Gillis Hooftman, or with a Calvinist like Hooftman's London representative Johan Radermacher.[69] Radermacher, after all, while still living in Antwerp, had collaborated with Plantijn on the profitable sale of two hundred Hebrew Bibles to the Jews of Morocco—reason for Hooftman to place an order for another five hundred copies.[70]

But disaster was just around the corner. The activities of a fringe group of Calvinist fanatics and dissatisfied noblemen, who for years had been rendering border areas unsafe and scouring the North Sea as freebooters, suddenly took on threatening proportions with their capture of Den Briel on April 1, 1572. In the same month Flushing also sided with the Prince of Orange. Almost overnight the rebels gained control over the mouths of the Maas and the Schelde.[71]

Slowly but surely choices had to be made. Like so many of his colleagues, Hooftman, as a Lutheran but also as a merchant, felt increasingly drawn to the side of the rebels. That he supported the Calvinists and was a friend of the Prince of Orange—an accusation noted already in 1566 in a secret report by the Spanish representative in Antwerp, Geronimo de Curiel—was now, in any case, a fact. He secretly dispatched a ship loaded with weapons to Flushing and arranged for the sale of cargo which the citizens of Flushing had seized from several Portuguese merchant vessels.[72]

An exploit of this kind certainly did him no harm. Years of constant warfare had brought about the collapse of the Antwerp stock exchange and credit system, but this meant that there were fortunes to be made in trading goods by anyone who still had capital.[73] In the same year he bought a country house with a sizable piece of land from the estate of the insurance agent Jan Henriques. It stood on the opposite bank of the Schelde, beside the ferry landing and directly across from the Wharf lined with his warehouses (see ill. 29).[74] A playground for his children? No doubt. But also a place of refuge if the situation became too dangerous in town, with its contingent of Spanish troops permanently garrisoned in the "Castle," the fortress which dominated the entire city. There was no greater threat to life and property than soldiers driven into a corner. And cornered they were, by the freebooting "Beggars," but especially by Philip's perennial shortage of funds owing to the sieges in Holland, the Turkish presence in the Mediterranean and dwindling revenues.

---

68   Hamilton 1981, p. 34-39, 65-67, 82; Moss 1981, p. 20.
69   Boumans 1954, p. 377; Ortelius 1887, p. xxvi; Bostoen 1984, p. 11; Heezen-Stoll 1990, p. 674.
70   Plantin 1 1883, p. 160; Voet 2 1972, p. 392-393.
71   Prims 8.2 1942, p. 236; Groenveld-Leeuwenberg 1979, p. 87-89.
72   Zweite 1980, p. 72; Berens 1968, p. 70; Smedt 1 1950, p. 402; see also Brulez 1959, p. 209.
73   Prims 8.2 1942, p. 168-169.
74   Couvreur 1975, p. 566.

29. *The Country House of Gillis Hooftman.*
     On the far left, on this side of the Schelde, stands the country house of Hooftman.
     Antwerp can be seen on the other side of the river, with the Wharf, site of his loading dock
     and warehouses.

Events gained momentum. New invasions by the two Oranges, Louis and William,
were fended off, and Spanish troops reconquered Haarlem. But the siege of Alkmaar
failed, and on the Zuider Zee Alva's fleet suffered a crushing defeat. This was the last
straw: Alva, the iron duke, who had gone so far as to place a bronze statue of himself in
the Antwerp castle with an inscription stating that he had restored peace and piety, now
had to admit that his policies had failed.[75] He resigned his post in November 1573.

But his successor, Don Luis de Requesens, formerly governor of Milan, was equally
incapable of turning the tide.[76] People lived from day to day. In April of 1574 the citizens
of Antwerp, including Hooftman, raised large sums of money to buy off four and a half
thousand foot soldiers who were threatening to plunder the city. One year later, in
March 1575, some light appeared on the horizon when peace negotiations were initiated.
In July they broke off, however, and September brought the second bankruptcy of the
Spanish state in twenty years. Repercussions followed quickly. In March 1576 the largest
banks were reported as ruined.[77] Requesens died that same month, far from peaceful
Milan which he had left against his will and, as he put it himself, with a broken heart.
From the moment that he heard of the Spanish bankruptcy his health began to decline.

Despite all this, there was still hope that everything would stabilize. But on June 30,
1576 the king's troops, fifty-three hundred strong, captured the city of Zierikzee and
marched on from there, plundering and looting their way into Flanders. The infantry
had received no pay for two full years, the cavalry for six. After ransacking the city of

---

75   Guicciardini 1612, p. 101.
76   Groenveld-Leeuwenberg 1979, p. 84, 90-95; Parker 1981, p. 149-156.
77   Prims 8.1 1941, p. 121-122; Prims 8.2 1942, p. 169.

Aalst, with its medieval town hall, bell tower and half-finished Martinus Church, they moved into Brabant, bringing with them all the horrors of an army on a rampage—rape, murder, arson. Entire villages went up in flames. In Brussels people gathered in anxious groups, swords in hand, staring at dark clouds of smoke billowing over the eastern horizon. From all directions farmers fled to the city, which soon fell prey to epidemics and serious food shortages.

Roads between cities were blocked and bridges destroyed in order to impede the progress of the mutineers; hastily the regional governments of Brabant and Flanders started recruiting troops. But what could they achieve against the experienced, well-trained and hardened soldiers of their own king? The troops of Brabant were thoroughly trounced near Tienen on September 14, and the Flemings could only expect a similar fate. The call for Orange grew steadily louder...[78]

During these same weeks Olivier Brunel was traveling with his Russian employers from Dordrecht to Antwerp—on his way to profitable business, but also to danger.

---

78   Groenveld-Leeuwenberg 1979, p. 97; Parker 1981, p. 157-170.

V   *The Islands*

– "Olivier Brunel."
– "Brunel! Is it possible, after all these years? Where have you been?"
– "In the Urals and Moscow, Kola and Dordrecht."

The return to Antwerp must have been a shock to Brunel. With its new town hall gleaming proudly in the sun the city was busier and more prosperous than his brightest memories had conjured up. But underneath all the bustle was a hint of something darker, a sudden look or turn of conversation that seemed to verge on fear. Only Hooftman was his usual unruffled self. In the high-ceilinged dining room of his house near the Castle he turned page after page of his atlas under the gaze of paintings which he had commissioned from Maarten de Vos on events in the life of Saint Paul—a monumental testimony to a faith in God (see ill. 30).[1]

30.   Maarten de Vos, *Paul on Malta* (1568).
      This painting was commissioned by Gillis Hooftman. The figures include likenesses of himself, Abraham Ortelius, and other contemporaries.

---

1   Zweite 1980, p. 73-84 and 267-269.

– "Look, America."

That, too, was amazing. Many years earlier, when Brunel had left Antwerp, it was assumed that Bacalaos, discovered by Cabot, was the coast of Asia, or at most some narrow strip of land. It was, to be sure, joined in the south to the America of the Spaniards—that much had been learned from Cabot's voyages along the eastern coast of the newly discovered land. But this did not rule out the likelihood of a northern passage. The gulf stream must have carved out an easy route somewhere.[2]

Ptolemy, however, had been greatly mistaken about the circumference of the earth, and entire generations of geographers had perpetuated his error.[3] Now there was a whole continent out there, as big as Europe and Asia together. Up to now, only the coast had been explored, but the land mass, according to the latest calculations, extended beyond the 260th degree of longitude.

Brunel stared. The entire east coast of the new world was filled with names of bays and settlements: Estotiland with the Baia do Serra, the Rio Nevado and the Rio de Tormenta, and farther south the Golfo di San Lorenzo and the settlements Hanguz, Canada and Roquelai (see ill. 31).[4]

– "Portuguese?"
– "That's what they say, yes, and French. Although Henry VIII also sent an expedition out there at the urging of Robert Thorne. That seems to have come to nothing, but now they're trying again."[5]

All that was left of Bacalaos was an island near the coast. But there were more surprises. In the ocean itself, between the old world and the new, were a large number of islands completely new to Brunel. Iceland, that was familiar. And Greenland, of course, although no one had known its exact location and it had generally been considered part of the polar land mass. But now, above it, even farther to the northwest, lay Grocland, and below it the rocky island of Huitsarc; in the northeast, at the entrance to the Arctic Ocean, were the two small islands Rustene and Santi, and the sea farther south, below Iceland, was dotted with more islands: Grisland and Frisland, Drogeo, Icaria, Neome, Podalida, and a good many more (see ill. 32).[6]

– "Yes, master Mercator hasn't been idle. Ortelius is greatly indebted to him, especially for his knowledge of the northern regions."[7]

Another map was brought out and unrolled on the table.

---

2   See for example Mercator 1538 (Nordenskiöld 1889 (1970), map nr. 43); Ptolemy 1540 (1966), "World Map;" Gemma Frisius 1551 (Nordenskiöld 1889 (1970), map nr. 44); cf. Morison 1978, p. 144-147.
3   Janssens-Uyttersprot 1990, p. 90.
4   Ortelius 1570 (1964), map 1 "Typus orbis terrarum."
5   Morison 1978, p. 76-103 and 140-273; Wallis 1984, p. 457-459.
6   Ortelius 1570 (1964), map 45 "Septentrionalium regionum descriptio."
7   Ortelius 1887, nr. 32, p. 73-74; Brandmair 1914, p. 24 Van der Krogt 1994, p. 98-102.

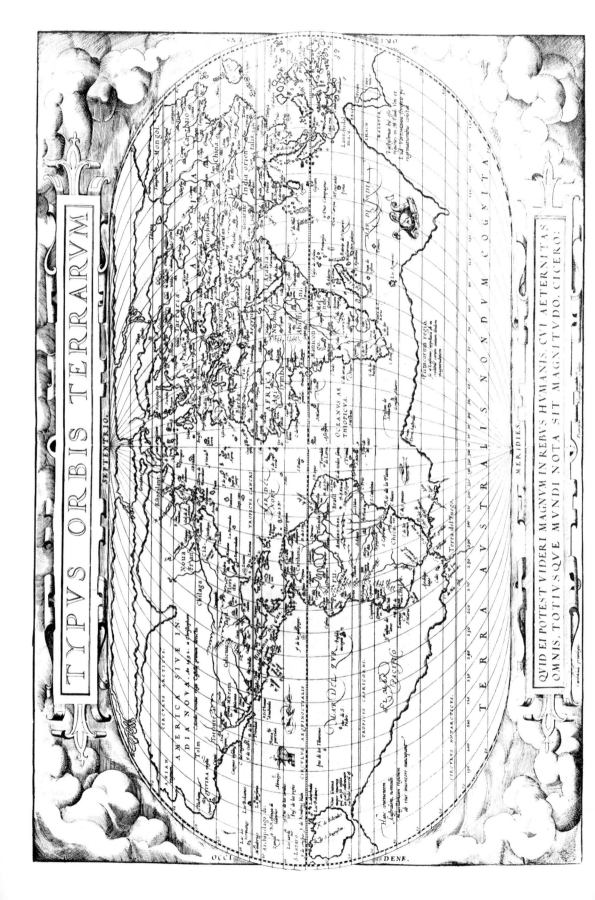

TYPVS ORBIS TERRARVM

SEPTENTRIO.

MERIDIES.

OCCI — DENS.

QVID EI POTEST VIDERI MAGNVM IN REBVS HVMANIS, CVI AETERNITAS OMNIS, TOTIVSQVE MVNDI NOTA SIT MAGNITVDO. CICERO:

31. (Illustration page 88.)
    Abraham Ortelius, *World Map* (1570).
    On the east coast of North America are the names of Portuguese and French settlements: Hanguz, Roquelai, Canada.

— "Look, this is the best one of all. One and a half by two meters of pure erudition, and useful for the navigator too. Plantijn has the monopoly on sales in the Netherlands, and I hear he's already sold one hundred and eighty-five of them. For three guilders a piece. Usually people would hesitate to spend that much on one map. It seems to be a limited edition, though, for obvious reasons."

— "What reasons?"

— "It's full of revolutionary new material—people usually prefer to buy something familiar. But in this case he wouldn't have had to worry. Look…"[8]

He pointed with a stubby finger:

— "Between Greenland and the north of the new world there's supposed to be a passage leading to the Strait of the Three Brothers, or the Anian Strait as they call it nowadays. From there you can sail down to Quivira on the west coast, the area explored by the Spanish. Don't you remember, Gemma Frisius already mentioned the Quii as the people Johannes Scolvuss ended up with. From there it should be just a short voyage to Zipangu and Cathay. Mercator is firmly convinced of this.[9] The English, too, for that matter. Some even say that in 1541 a ship full of goods and with paintings of exotic birds on its sails anchored on the south side of the Strait of the Three Brothers. With sign language the crew made it clear that they had come from Cathay and that it had taken them thirty days."[10]

— "And you call that a short voyage?"

— "A lot shorter in any case than via the Strait of Magellan. That's fifteen thousand miles, not counting storms and currents which make the passage all but impossible.[11] No, I can understand those Englishmen. Jenkinson seems dissatisfied with the results in Russia and has found a rich nobleman to finance it all, and John Dee himself has given nautical advice.[12] On June 7th they left with three ships under the command of Martin Frobisher, and they were already back by October 2nd. With a large lump of gold and with a native who looked just like a Tartar."[13]

— "What exactly did he look like?"

— "A fat body, short legs and a broad dark face with small eyes, a thin black beard and long pitch-black hair tied together above his forehead."[14]

---

8   Denucé 2 1913, p. 284-285; Voet 1962, p. 173-177 and 215-217; Mercator 1569 (1961), "Introduction," p. 11 and p. 18-19.

9   Skelton 1962, p. 165-166; Mercator 1569 (1961), leaf 8.

10 *State Papers* 1862, p. 11, nr. 21.

11 *State Papers* 1862, p. 11, nr. 23; cf. Morison 1978, p. 600-602 and 612.

12 Wallis 1984, p. 459; State Papers 1862, p. 13, nr. 27.

13 Morison 1978, p. 277-284; Wallis 1984, p. 460-462.

14 *State Papers* 1862, p. 13-14, nr. 27.

32. (Illustration page 90.)
    Abraham Ortelius, *The Northern Lands* (1570).
    Following the example set by Mercator on his world map of 1569, Ortelius fills the northern ocean with islands mentioned in old travel accounts, most of which were imaginary: Grocland, Icaria, Drogeo, Frisland, Grisland, Neome, Podalida and, above Norway, Santi and Rustene. The peninsula on the American mainland previously known as Bacalaos is here called Estotiland. Between Iceland and Greenland lies the rock island of Huitsarc.

– "English bluff. Tartars don't look like that, Jenkinson knows that as well as I do. As far as the Russian trade is concerned, he's just disappointed that the tsar is threatening to rescind the English monopoly and allow others into the White Sea.[15] Because there are good profits to be made there, you can be sure of that— hides, salmon, tallow—better than in the so-called new world."

But on Sunday, November 4, 1576, when the negotiations in Ghent aimed at reaching an agreement with the Prince of Orange had been under way for more than two weeks,[16] all hell broke loose in Antwerp. It had begun that previous Friday. The Spanish soldiers quartered in the Castle were making louder and louder demands for pay, while the regional troops approached the city from the other side. Spanish and Italian merchants had started sending their families and possessions to the safety of the Castle, but the rest of the city went about daily life as usual.

That morning, at ten o'clock, the regional troops were admitted to the city through the Kipdorp Gate on the northeast side (see ill. 33). They marched south, directly toward the Castle. There, on the edge of the parade grounds, they started improvising barricades between the St. George Gate on the east side and the Kronenburg Gate on the Schelde. Wool and hop sacks, empty barrels, even old chairs were used. And men, women, boys, and girls were all enlisted to help dig trenches. The fog was so thick that no one in the Castle could see what was going on. Later that night the soldiers finally noticed, and started shooting. They continued the entire next day, and into the afternoon of the day following, Sunday. Straight through the houses they shot, killing many citizens.

On Sunday morning mutinous troops from Aalst and Maastricht came to reinforce the Spaniards. They entered the Castle through the back gate and immediately left from the front to storm the street fortifications. Heavy fighting continued for hours. Dead bodies littered the streets. Eventually the barricades were crushed and the troops moved on into the city, down St. George Street and Beguine Street, Walloon Street and Cloister Street. Bells tolled. Citizens came rushing from their houses with guns and swords in their hands. But further fighting was useless.

Driving the defenders back, the troops managed to reach the Great Market Square. Marksmen still offered some resistance from inside the new city hall, but were soon forced to leap from windows when the building was set ablaze. They moved on, to the north side of town where fleeing citizens made desperate attempts with ropes and poles

---

15   Willan 1968, p. 128.
16   Groenveld-Leeuwenberg 1979, p. 98-100.

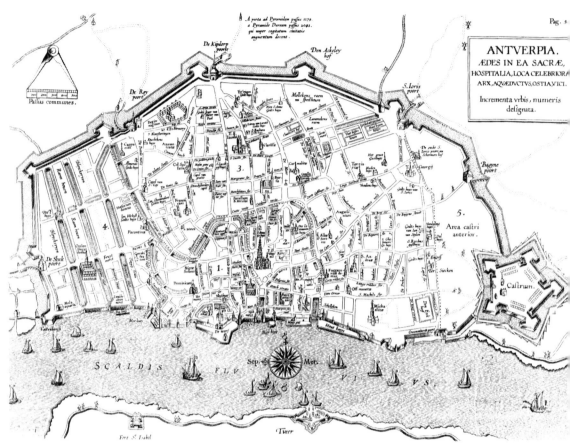

33. *Antwerp and the Spanish Fury.*
From the Castle the soldiers stormed through St. George Street, Beguine Street, Walloon
Street and Cloister Street, plundering and burning their way into the city. The area around
the Great Market—Fair Street, Silver Street, Cheese Street, Sugar Row, Flax Market and a
part of High Street—went up in flames. The far end of Cloister Street, near the Castle, suffered the same fate.

to scramble over the walls and escape into the open fields, or to reach the Schelde from
the canals in Newtown. Overloaded boats capsized and many drowned.

Then, on Sunday evening, after the last resistance had been broken, the plundering
started and did not stop until the following Thursday. Doors were rammed or shot
open and soldiers stormed into houses with rapiers in hand. Money was demanded,
large amounts of it, and when they had taken it all they still wanted more. House after
house went up in flames, as reprisals for those unable to pay. Virtually the entire area
around the Great Market—Fair Street, Silver Street, Cheese Street, Sugar Row, Flax
Market, half of High Street—and in the southern part of the city everything around the
far end of Cloister Street, was reduced to ashes.

At least five hundred houses were destroyed, and about nine hundred more were seriously damaged. Some reports mentioned five thousand dead, others eighteen thousand. Days later bodies were still being pulled from the rubble.[17] It was hardly surprising that people began to wonder whether 1576, rather than 1556 or 1566, was to be the magical year in which the Antichrist would come to destroy unrepentant sinners. Despite all that followed—a general agreement between the regions and the Prince of Orange that the foreign troops would be required to leave the country, the subsequent withdrawal of the Spanish troops and the appointment of the king's half-brother, Don Juan, as the latest in the rapid succession of governors, and finally, in September 1577, the return of William of Orange to Antwerp[18]—the city would never be the same again.

But business continued. A short three months after the devastation, with the smell of soot and scorched mortar still hanging in the streets, Abraham Ortelius set out for London. In January, John Dee had written to him about the plans for Frobisher's second voyage, and some believed that his only reason for visiting London was to find out the details.[19]

There was still so much to discover. Uncharted were not only the northern regions of America; in the great ocean itself nearly all the new islands pictured on Mercator's world map were still waiting to be explored. The sea route to Greenland remained a matter of great uncertainty. And even Iceland, where for centuries ships had been taking on cargoes of butter and dried fish,[20] was the subject of strange tales.

-   "Take Olaus Magnus' book about the northern lands, for example. The man is a Swede himself, but the nonsense he writes… Before Plantijn could publish a respectable new edition, our municipal secretary Cornelius Grapheus kept busy right up to his death editing out all the outdated and useless material trotted out by that would-be archbishop."[21]
-   "Would-be?"
-   "Yes, of course. The Pope may have appointed him, but he never went back to Sweden. What was he supposed to do there after the whole country turned Lutheran?[22] In any case, the size of the book is much more manageable now and its contents are more useful, but it's a strange world, nevertheless."

And so it was. If one country confirmed Postel's theory that Satan lay chained in the north and that demonic powers of all sorts manifested themselves there, it was Iceland. Nature itself was in the thrall of these forces. The mountain tops were covered with perpetual snow while the earth at their feet hissed and bubbled with subterranean fires which could break forth at any moment, as the eruptions of 1558 had shown.[23] Dotting the land-

17   Prims 8.1 1942, p. 130-133; Ortelius 1887, nr. 64, p. 145-153.
18   Prims 8.1 1941, p. 134-140; Parker 1981, p. 172-177.
19   Ortelius 1887, nr. 67, p. 160 and nr. 68, p. 161.
20   Magnus 1558, p. 176 recto-verso.
21   Magnus 1558, commission Plantijn, p. a 2 verso. For Grapheus' contribution see Magnus 1562, title page, and Nauwelaerts 1983, p. 319.
22   Thoroddsen 1 1897, p. 124; Knauer 1981, p. 23-24; Johannesson 1991, p. 141-149.
23   Arngrimus Ionas Islandus, in Hakluyt 1 1598, p. 557.

scape were ponds of steaming green water which tasted of sulphur, with clouds of mosquitos hovering over them. In the distance rose black slopes covered with ash, and behind them, at higher altitudes, enormous sheets of ice stood like white walls against the sky.

Nothing grew there—no trees, no grain—except scattered patches of grass in the south. The people used whale ribs to build their dwellings. Their food consisted of fish dried on rocks, and whatever they managed to trade with merchants who came by ship from Denmark, or from Germany and England, or occasionally from the Netherlands.

All this was already known in the eleventh century from the writings of Adam of Bremen, and similar reports were still coming back in the sixteenth century.[24] None of it was too hard to believe, but then there were all those other tales as well. Certain springs found there could supposedly turn everything to stone, and others were so poisonous that anyone who drank from them would immediately fall down dead; there were hot water geysers and springs flowing with beer.[25] Among the mountains and the rocks flowed rivers of churning ice which in the course of time would carry the bodies of people who had fallen into crevices back to the surface.[26] The land was continually swept by a northwest wind so powerful that it could throw fully armored men from their horses or blow the water out from under ships at sea, leaving them high and dry in mid-air.[27]

But worst of all was Mount Hekla, which, like Etna in Italy, was continually on fire. It was said to be the gateway to purgatory, where souls went to be purified after death (see ill. 34). That was undoubtedly nonsense dreamt up by some medieval Pope,[28] because the same story was told about a cave in Ireland, formerly thought to be the end of the world and the place where St. Patrick had been given a glimpse of purgatory.[29] And yet…

"Woe, woe is me," had been heard there, and the gnashing of teeth. From two sides of the mountain sprang rivers, one black and burning, the other ice cold, and in these the souls of the dead were tormented. Chunks of blazing wood went flying through the air as well as flaming birds which rose out of the crater and swooped, screeching, through the sky.

All this had been described by St. Brendan centuries earlier.[30] And later the monk Alberich from the Cistercian monastery in Trois Fontaines near Strasbourg had written that in the year 1134, during the battle of Fode Bay in southern Sweden, which claimed the lives of five bishops as well as the son of King Niels the Great, shepherds in Iceland had heard black birds crying as they flew, "Woe, woe is us, what have we done? Oh woe, what has befallen us?" And they had seen how other gigantic birds resembling griffins had attacked them and driven them all into the Icelandic inferno. And in the year 1341 souls in the form of loudly screeching birds had been seen flying through the flames erupting from Hekla.[31]

24   Adam von Bremen 1917, p. 272 (IV.xxxvi); Nordenskiöld 1889 (1970), p. 59, ill. 32; cf. Knauer 1981, p. 35-36.
25   Knauer 1981, p. 35; cf. Saxo 1 1979, p. 7-8 and Thoroddsen 1 1897, p. 125.
26   Saxo 1 1979, p. 8.
27   Magnus 1558, p. 2 verso - 3 recto.
28   Namely Gregory the Great (sixth century). See Bächtold-Stäubli 4 1931-32, col. 223.
29   *Decleringe* 1 1983, p. 49, 2 1983, p. 127-128.
30   Brandaan 1978, p. 87 and p. 148-151.
31   Maurer 1894, p. 258-259.

De ſecreta natura quorundam montium.

34. *The Volcanoes on Iceland.*
The mountain in the middle is Hekla, with snow ("nix") covering its peak and flames at its base. There one can see the entrance to the underworld ("chaos").

A reliable authority like Saxo had, it is true, pointed out that all those strange creaking sounds came from ice floes being pushed up against the rocks.[32] Writers of the time like Ziegler and Sebastian Münster seemed to consider this the more plausible explanation, but in spite of that they, too, repeated tales about people who had drowned but who later appeared to passers-by as if they were still alive; with a sigh they would dissolve into thin air as soon as anyone tried to touch them. Tales like these were found in Olaus.[33]

And what was to be made of the story of a ship which, while sailing from Iceland with a strong tailing wind, was passed by another ship sailing with the speed of a storm—believe it or not—straight into the gale. When they called out, "Where do you come from?" the captain answered, "From the Bishop of Bremen." And when they shouted, "Where are you going?" the answer was "To Hekla, to Hekla."[34]

But the people, Olaus wrote, were good Christians, averse to all luxury. From the earliest times amazed writers had testified about how contented and happy they were, how full of brotherly love, how they shared everything, both amongst themselves and with strangers.[35] They had their own script which they had used for centuries to record the brave deeds of their countrymen, and now, too, they were always writing down the latest events. To make it all easier to remember they turned it into songs and refrains which they chiseled into the rocks above the sea.[36]

---

32   Saxo 1 1979, p. 8.
33   Zieglerus-Krantzius 1583, p. 480; Münster 1550 (1968), p. 985; Magnus 1558, p. 13 recto-verso.
34   Arngrimus Ionas Islandus, in Hakluyt 1 1598, p. 560.
35   Adam von Bremen 1917, p. 272-273 (IV.xxxvi).
36   Magnus 1558, p. 12 verso - 13 recto.

This was all quite different from the old wives' tales of Pliny about islands in the north where the natives were born with horses' hooves instead of feet, or with ears so long that they covered their entire body, making clothes unnecessary.[37] No, Postel had been right when he wrote that the source of good had to be near that of evil, and that the farther north one went the more fair-minded the people were.

And beyond Iceland? Farther north there was Greenland, but Greenland had gotten lost.

- "Officially at least."
- "What do you mean? Are there people who…"
- "Who knows. I can't say. But you'll always find some seamen who'll risk sailing where others never go."
- "I've heard that the Danish king thinks the death penalty is not too severe a punishment for people who infringe on his monopoly."
- "The Danish king himself hasn't managed to reopen the trade route."
- "I've also heard that no one is living there anymore except the Pygmies, called Skraelings. Wiped out, all of them, murdered by the Skraelings, they say.[38] So who would there be to trade with?"
- "Well, I've heard that there are people living there, small as Pygmies but of Norwegian stock.[39] Just rumors, of course. Whoever might be trading with them behind the back of the Danish king certainly wouldn't let it be known. But I can assure you in any case that the people living there have not turned green from the sea water but from malnutrition and disease.[40] The Danish kings and their advisors stopped sending provisions but continued to forbid private trade—they'll have to answer to their Maker for that someday."

Most important now was to realize that the northernmost regions were not necessarily too cold to be inhabitable, as some people claimed. The learned geographer Jakob Ziegler had already been very emphatic on this point. And although he might have been wrong about Greenland being the same as the newly discovered land of Bacalaos—he, along with many other scholars in Germany, believed that there was one self-contained polar land mass extending from Lapland to Biarmaland[41]—this did not mean he was wrong on the question of its habitability. He had pointed out the abundance of fish in the sea and wild animals on land. What is more, he had come with scientific arguments which were difficult to refute, based as they were on the characteristics of the four elements themselves, air, water, earth, and fire.

Since each element had to be found in close proximity to that which most resembled it—there were, as everyone knew, no incompatibilities in nature—water was the thickest, and therefore the saltiest, in those places where it bordered on earth. For salt was

---

37   Pliny 2 1969, p. 192-193 (IV.xiii.95); Solinus 1572, p. 124 (xxii).
38   Hennig 3 1953, p. 437-441.
39   Hennig 3 1953, p. 451-455.
40   Adam von Bremen 1917, p. 274 (IV.xxxvii); Krantzius 1583, p. 331; Hennig 3 1953, p. 448.
41   Zieglerus-Krantzius 1583, p. 480; Nordenskiöld 1889 (1970), p. 576, illus. 31; Münster 1550 (1968), p. 987.

the substance which thickened water. Salt, according to Pliny, imparted an oily or fatty quality, and oil with its potential for warmth was closely related to fire. This meant that in areas where the sea reached into the land in the form of countless inlets the salt content would stimulate warmth and the fattiness fertility. This mutual penetration of water and earth would also moderate the temperature of the air. And to the extent that there was still some extreme cold, nature had provided her creatures with deep caves and thick coats of fur or, in the case of human beings, with the strength to hunt as well as the intelligence and skill to fabricate clothing, heated dwellings, featherbeds.[42]

According to Ziegler, Greenland had formerly produced large quantities of butter and cheese for export, but now only Lapps lived there, the same as those found along the northern coast of the European continent between North Cape and the Ob'. And they were equally adept at magic: with their songs they conjured up storms and capsized ships in order to take possession of the cargo. At times Pygmies also came south from the uncharted land beneath the pole. A rapacious tribe, no larger than ten-year-old children, but known for being as vicious as they were small.[43]

This was reliable information, very different from Olaus Magnus' pretentious display of erudition. How could anyone believe all his stories, not only that these fearless pygmies would attack people of normal size but also that every spring they would arm themselves with spears, mount rams and goats and travel south in battle array to feast for three months on the eggs and chicks of cranes (see ill. 35). Only with this show of force could they fend off attacks by the furious birds.

He had taken this story from Pliny and attempted to make it more credible by alluding to Solinus, who with his penchant for even wilder fantasies, had maintained

35. *Battle between the Pygmies and the Cranes.*
Olaus Magnus took this story by Pliny and applied it to the Eskimos, known since Claudius Clavus as "Pygmies."

---

42   Zieglerus-Krantzius 1583, p. 477-478.
43   Zieglerus-Krantzius 1583, p. 479-480; Nordenskiöld 1889 (1970), p. 49, ill. 27.

LIBER   SECVNDVS

36. *Flotsam and Huts Made of Whale Ribs.*
     The Pygmies on Greenland were said to live in huts like these, covered with twigs and
     moss.

that a flock of cranes had once driven the Pygmies out of the city of Gerania, which means "pelican bill." As for the cranes—probably geese or swans—Olaus told how they prepared for their flight to the north by swallowing sand and stones for ballast to keep them from being blown off course by storms, and how they vomited everything out again upon reaching their destination.[44]

All nonsense, of course, rightly deleted by Cornelius Grapheus. But it was probably true that there, as in Iceland, the houses were built of whale ribs covered with twigs and moss, and that to seamen in the occasional ship passing in the distance they looked like overturned boats (see ill. 36). Also true, no doubt, was that they had leather boats which could be used under water as well as on the surface; this was how they managed to bore holes into the underside of passing ships and cause them to sink, then take the cargo as booty.[45] This elusive kind of danger, looming suddenly out of nowhere, from behind a wave or an ice floe, was familiar to Brunel. He had seen these people in Kola, and later near Vaygach. And it proved once again that Claudius Clavus and Ziegler and Münster, and Olaus Magnus as well, had been right when they claimed that Greenland extended to Vardöhus and beyond.[46] However, there could have been water in between, for these natives would just as readily take their boats ten or twenty miles out to sea, out of sight of land, as they would venture into channels through pack ice. As if it was not already the most treacherous sea imaginable, with its invisible reefs and whirlpools, and its storms which gathered and burst before you realized it, filling the water, which moments before had seemed smooth and clear, with drifting ice.

The biggest problem was how to get there. Nowhere was the sea so perilous as northwest of Norway, full of whirlpools with uprooted trees spinning around in them, half-rotten perhaps, but still capable of knocking a hole in the hull of a ship. Most

---

44   Magnus 1555, p. 70-71 (not in Magnus 1558).
45   Magnus 1555, p. 68; cf. also Magnus 1558, p. 16 verso.
46   Magnus 1555, p. 69 (not in Magnus 1558).

feared was the one due west of Lofoten. This was the maelstrom which medieval scholars like Paulus Diaconus and Giraldus identified as the one through which all the sea currents were sucked inside the earth. They were mistaken, because that vortex had to be located much farther north. But here, too, navigators were forced to keep changing course, first sailing in one direction and then in the other to avoid difficulties. As if that were not enough, there were violent storms, especially around the full moon, which every sailor dreaded.[47]

On that sort of pale moonlit night, when a ship would be carried to the crest of a high wave only to be hurled down again into the black depths, you might catch a glimpse of the wizard Holler riding the seas astride the skeleton of a giant fish, his cloak billowing like a sail in the wind.[48] Then a sailor would make the sign of the cross and curse the day that he had set foot on board.

But those who made it past this maelstrom would be en route to the new world, even though no one knew exactly what they would find there.[49]

The route… There were sailing instructions, or at least rumors of sailing instructions. Brunel remembered the words of a sailor from Hamburg:

– "In good weather, two-thirds of the way between Ireland and Iceland, you can see both Snaevelsjokel on Iceland and Huitsarc on Greenland. They say that it's no more than thirty sea weeks, that's one hundred eighty miles, between those two lands. If the current is from the north you have to be careful that it doesn't carry you to Ireland, but if it's from the south you have to set a southwest course when you see Huitsarc stretching out in the north.[50]

Ziegler also wrote about Huitsarc, or Witsarc, the "white shirt" on Greenland, undoubtedly a glacier like the *jokels* of Iceland which extended high into the sky, some of them even above the clouds. He mentioned a peninsula or a cape, and his map showed three mountain tops half submerged in the sea.[51]

But Olaus maintained that Huitsarc was a rocky island midway between Iceland and Greenland. Two notorious pirates, Pining and Pothorst, had supposedly taken refuge there around 1494 after the kings of the northern countries had jointly exiled them from all human society as punishment for their heinous crimes. From this island they waylaid all the ships which came into view. High on a rock jutting out of the sea they had constructed a navigation symbol from lead: rosette-shaped, like a compass, it was a sign to all pirates for miles around that they could expand their freebooting in that direction to good advantage (see ill. 37).[52]

---

47   Magnus 1555, p. 69; cf. Magnus 1558, p. 15 verso; Hennig 3 1953, p. 318.
48   Magnus 1558, p. 40 recto.
49   Magnus 1555, p. 69 (not in Magnus 1558).
50   Hennig 3 1953, p. 435-436; Burger 1928, p. 232.
51   Zieglerus-Krantzius 1583, p. 479; and Nordenskiöld 1889 (1970), p. 57, ill. 31.
52   Magnus 1555, p. 70 (not in Magnus 1558).

37. *The Navigation Symbol on Huitsarc.*

– "But Grapheus took that out, too, and rightly so. Didrik Pining a pirate, the very idea!"

He and Pothorst had actually erected that symbol as a warning against Greenland pirates who made their forays in those unlikely little boats. They were German seamen who had set out in the service of King Christian I of Denmark to discover new lands and to rediscover Greenland. And they were no ordinary seamen: Pining had become governor of Iceland and later commander of Vardohüs; and although Pothorst was not as famous, his portrait was said to hang in the Maria Church of Elsinore.[53]

Whether the rock was called Huitsarc or not, and whether the navigation symbol was meant as a warning for or against pirates, it was very likely a sign pointing the way to Greenland. That was how they did things up north. There was a sign like this at North Cape, as well, cut high into the rock of a cliff face, also in the form of a compass.[54]

The Danish king was not the only one bent on finding Greenland. Queen Elizabeth of England was interested as well, and for good reason. Shortly after being visited by Ortelius, John Dee had received a letter from his old friend Mercator, explaining how he had obtained the information about the polar regions which appeared on his world map.[55] Most of it came in the last analysis from the mysterious *Inventio Fortunata*, the book which Johannes Ruysch had used previously as the basis for his world map. Mercator's direct source, the travel account of a certain Jacobus Cnoyen from 's Hertogenbosch, had since disappeared without a trace. He attempted to retrieve the work, which he had once had on loan. In vain. Fortunately, however, he had copied some of the most important passages.[56] Above the northern coast of Norway, beyond the Sucking Sea,

---

53   Hennig 4 1956, p. 247-258; Dreyer-Eimbcke 1994, p.137.
54   Hennig 4 1956, p. 260.
55   Skelton 1962, p. 163; Dreyer-Eimbcke 1994, p. 150-154.
56   Durme 1959, nr. 143, p. 159; Taylor 1956, p. 56-58.

there was supposedly the land of Obscure as well as three other polar islands. Surrounding them at the seventy-eighth parallel was a mountain range intersected by gulf streams too powerful for any ship to navigate. Around the pole lay open water, and precisely in the middle stood a gleaming black rock, thirty-three miles in circumference. All this he had indicated on his map.

But Cnoyen also related that King Arthur of Britain had sent an army on a northern expedition, and they had found another island beyond Greenland called Grocland. Arthur had subjugated all the islands between Scotland and Grocland. But four thousand of his best men were lost somewhere in the Sucking Sea on the far side of Grocland. A few seem to have survived, however, eking out an existence in that region together with the indigenous Pygmies. At least a story was told that eight of their descendants, including two priests, had found their way to the Norwegian court. They reported seeing giants on Grocland, thirty-three feet tall, eighteen hundred men and four hundred women.

One of these descendants had in his possession a kind of astrolabe which he claimed to have obtained from the Oxford monk who wrote the *Inventio Fortunata*.[57] In Dee's opinion this had to be the mathematician Nicholas van Lynn, although his identity remained uncertain.[58] In any case, this man must have penetrated even farther north, to judge from his knowledge of the polar islands and the gulf streams.

On the eastern polar island he had encountered people, a group of twenty-three including sixteen women, none of them more than four feet tall but beyond all doubt members of the human race. Elsewhere he had seen tree trunks as well as planks and beams from ships all piled up in a way which was obviously the work of human beings. But they had apparently left the area or died out. He had also visited the western island, which proved to have the best land and healthiest climate of the entire north, but he found no trace of living creatures there. All that land was densely forested and flat, without a single mountain except for the surrounding range.[59]

- "And Elizabeth?"
- "Elizabeth can all too easily use the evidence of King Arthur's conquests to support her claim to sovereignty over everything between Scotland and the pole.[60] It seems she is even planning to give Frobisher seven convicts to take along on his voyage this year. The idea is that he'll drop them in Frisland to collect information about the land and its inhabitants."[61]
- "Frisland?"
- "Yes, another one of those islands discovered two hundred years ago, then completely forgotten. Only in this century, now that people are seriously exploring the earth, do you find it on maps. High time that someone went there and drew them into the community of civilized peoples. Just imagine, until now we only knew about it from some letters found by a child playing in an attic. He even

57   Durme 1959, nr. 114 b, p. 132-135.
58   Hakluyt 1 1598, p. 121-122; Vaughan 1982, p. 321.
59   Durme 1959, nr. 114 b, p. 135-139.
60   Skelton 1962, p. 166-167; French 1984, p. 195-198.
61   State papers 1862, p. 20, nr. 37.

seems to have torn them up at first; only later, as an adult, did he realize their importance. He then did his best to reconstruct everything, also published a map of the area that he found among the family documents."[62]

- "Quite a story."
- "Certainly, but such things do happen…"

It was in the year 1380, after the war with Genoa, that the brave and rich knight Nicolò Zeno was gripped with a longing to see the world and to learn about the languages and customs of foreign peoples—this, he thought, would make him better able to serve his fatherland and bring him personal glory. He equipped a ship at his own expense and set out eastward. Once past the Strait of Gibraltar he altered his course, sailing north for days, with the intention of reaching Flanders and England.

But a tremendous storm overtook him. For days on end he was swept along by wind and waves, with no idea where he was going. Finally, together with his crew and most of his cargo, he was washed safely ashore on the island of Frisland (see ill. 38). The castaways hardly had firm ground beneath their feet when they were attacked by a large group of islanders. There would have been little hope of escape if an important knight passing by had not heard their shouts and hurried to their rescue.

In Latin he asked where they had come from, and when he heard that they were from Italy he promised them protection. As it turned out he was the lord of an island group neighboring Frisland on the south, as well as the duke of Sorano, near Scotland. His name was Zichmi. He was a brave man, renowned for his military exploits. In the preceding year he had defeated the king of Norway, and now he had brought his men here to conquer Frisland, an island somewhat larger than Ireland. When he realized that Nicolò was an experienced seaman and soldier he took him and his men into his own service and sent them in his ships to the western side of the island.

There were thirteen ships in all, two galleys and the rest small barks. The sea in that area was full of sandbanks and rocky reefs, and if Nicolò and his Venetian sailors had not served as pilots, the entire fleet would certainly have been lost, so inexperienced were Zichmi's crew by comparison.

- "Really, now—what about all those earlier conquests? The islanders must have known those seas like the backs of their hands?"

Without much difficulty they took possession of several small islands and then set course for the harbor of Sanestol on Frisland itself to rendezvous with Zichmi, who had been fighting his way over land. From there they sailed on, conquering more islands and other parts of Frisland for Zichmi. Triumphantly they returned to the capital city, also called Frisland, on the eastern side of the island. To make a long story short, the entire population eventually surrendered and accepted Zichmi as their ruler. And Zichmi thanked Nicolò for saving his fleet, dubbed him a knight and presented him and his men with precious gifts.

---

62   Zeno-Major 1873, p. 3-4 and p. 34-35; Karrow 1993, p. 600-602.

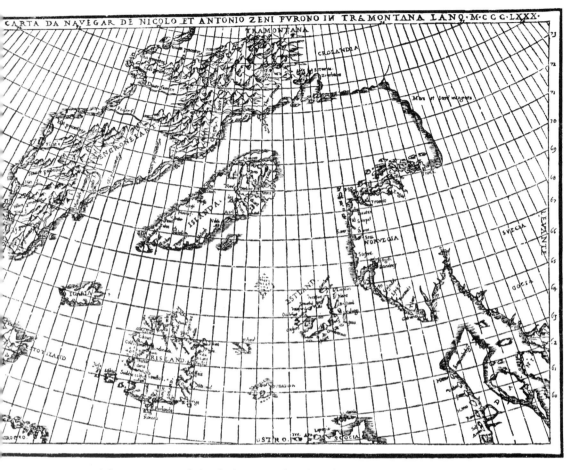

38. *Map of the Journeys made by the Zeno Brothers* (1561).
The imaginary islands shown here—Icaria, Drogeo, Frisland, Grisland, Neome and
Podalida, as well as Estotiland—would later be incorporated by Mercator into his world
map of 1569.

    The capital city of Frisland was located on a bay so full of fish—with such promise
of profit—that it attracted ships from Flanders, Brittany, England, Scotland, Norway
and Denmark. With one of those ships Nicolò sent a letter urging his brother, Antonio,
to come and join him. And Antonio, as eager to go out and see the world as his brother
had been, bought a ship and set sail for Frisland, where he remained for fourteen years.
But Nicolò, who had in the meantime been appointed admiral, set out after Antonio's
arrival to conquer Estland, which lay between Frisland and Norway.
    That mission failed. Nicolò's men managed to wreak considerable destruction on
the island, but upon hearing that the king of Norway was approaching with a large
fleet, they fled headlong into a storm. Several of their ships were driven onto sandbanks
and lost; the rest ended up on Grisland, a large uninhabited island farther north. Later
they heard from other passing ships that the storm had also devastated the fleet of the

Norwegian king, leaving no survivors. For Zichmi this was reason enough to launch an attack on Iceland, which until then had been subject to the king of Norway. But this mission also failed. The island was much too well fortified and armed. His troops managed to occupy only seven small islands, and on one of them they built a fort. Zichmi returned to Frisland, but Nicolò remained there with a small group of men, some boats and supplies, for he was determined to sail farther north the following year.

In July of the next year he set out with three barks, steering a northern course until he came to Greenland. There he found a Dominican monastery and a church dedicated to St. Thomas. This was near a mountain which, like Etna and Vesuvius, spewed fire. They found hot water springs there as well. The monks led the water through underground conduits to keep it from cooling off, and in this way heated the church, the monastery and their cells. When the water finally reached the monastery kitchen it was still so hot that no fire was needed to cook their food. They baked their bread by putting dough into copper pots and placing them in the water.

The pipes eventually led into a large copper kettle which stood in the middle of a fountain in the entrance hall of the monastery. This provided warm water for the personal needs of the monks and their gardens. By covering the gardens in the winter to protect them from the snow and cold, and sprinkling them with warm water, they managed to produce flowers, fruit and vegetables of all sorts. The natives there believed the monks to be gods and brought them gifts of chicken and meat and showed them all the honor to which gods were entitled.

- "That's no different from anywhere else. I've never yet met a monk who didn't think he was a god."
- "True enough."

The monks had built their cloister of lava from the volcano. By throwing water on it, they dissolved it into a white limestone from which they made rock-hard bricks. The arches which they constructed from these bricks were so light that they needed no support, and they were unsurpassed in beauty and durability. At the point where the hot water flowed into the sea there was a broad harbor which never froze over; it attracted so many birds and fish that they could be caught in unlimited numbers. In the summer many ships came from neighboring islands, as well as from North Cape and Trondheim in Norway, bringing necessary supplies in exchange for a wide variety of wild animal hides. There were always ships in the harbor waiting for the ice farther out at sea to melt or for a storm to abate.

Living around the monastery were a large number of people who earned their living from building, fishing and a thousand other occupations. Workmen aplenty. They lived in little round houses, twenty-five feet in diameter at the base and gradually narrowing toward the top where a small hole let in light and air. Their boats were made of the bones and skins of fish sewn together, and were so strong that even crashing against rocks would not break them. It was almost beyond belief, the way these people secured themselves inside their boats in bad weather and set out to sea without the least sign of fear. In the middle of the boat they attached a kind of sleeve to a hole in the bottom. In it they collected the water which washed into the boat, and when the sleeve was full they tied it firmly at the top, opened the bottom and forced the water back into the sea. They did this as often as necessary, without any peril to themselves.

All this Nicolò had seen and described. But despite all the comforts, he eventually fell ill from the cold. He returned to Frisland and died there. And Antonio inherited all his wealth and power.

Antonio would have preferred to return to Italy, but Zichmi would not hear of it, determined as he was to rule the sea. He insisted that Antonio come along on an expedition westward, to Estotiland, where twenty-six years earlier a few fishermen had ended up after drifting one thousand miles off course. One of them had returned years later with stories about a splendid, densely populated city and its friendly inhabitants.

The king of Estotiland had summoned all his interpreters in his attempt to understand the castaways, but none of them spoke a familiar language, with the exception of one man, also stranded there after a shipwreck, who spoke Latin. They stayed there for five years. It was a somewhat smaller island than Iceland, but more fertile and prosperous. In the middle rose a high mountain, the source of four rivers which supplied water to the entire area. The inhabitants were intelligent and cultivated, and in times long past they must have had contact with European civilization, for the king's library included Latin books which no one was able to read anymore.

Farther to the south was a large, densely populated land, rich in gold and covered by vast forests. And even farther south was an island called Drogeo. Because the fishermen were able to navigate with a compass, the king had sent them there with twelve boats. But after being washed ashore by a storm, most of them were captured and eaten by the natives, cannibals who considered human flesh a delicacy.

- – "So it was America."
- – "Maybe."
- – "The Grypes or Hyperboreans of Doctor Becanus, no doubt?"
- – "Let's just say Indians. It's possible, but who knows how many other kinds of lands and peoples there might be? Only in the last few years has it become clear how little we know. Next to nothing."

According to that fisherman it was a vast land, inhabited by savages who lived from their hunting but who had no idea that the hides of the animals which they caught could be used to protect themselves from the cold.

Eventually this man managed to escape and return via Drogeo and Estotiland to Frisland. Upon hearing the story of his experiences Zichmi resolved to send an expedition in that direction. And now that he had his Venetian admiral, he believed that the moment had come.

They set out with a large number of ships. In spite of Antonio's presence Zichmi himself took command of the fleet. From the start it was an ill-fated venture. The fisherman who was to be their guide died three days before their departure, but Zichmi insisted on going through with the plans. Once at sea they were surprised by a terrible storm.

- – "Another one?"
- – "It's a bad area for storms, everyone knows that."

For eight days they had no idea where they were being driven, and many of the ships were lost. Finally they came to the island Icaria, named after its first king, Icarus, son of Dedalus, king of Scotland.

- – "Oh, sure."
- – "Yes, and a lot of interesting things have been reported about that place. For example, that they still feel bound to the laws of their first king, who drowned in the sea there; that's why it's called the Icarian Sea."
- – "Never heard of it."
- – "And that they would rather die than accept another ruler."

A large crowd of furious islanders met them and forced them to flee. With difficulty they replenished their supplies of water and wood in a bay on the east side of the island. Meanwhile the natives warned one another with smoke signals from the surrounding hilltops, then rushed down the slopes brandishing bows and arrows. Many of the crew died in the ambush before they could escape in their boats.

For ten days they struggled between sandbanks and reefs, and every time they were driven toward the shore they saw the natives standing on the hills, shouting and shooting arrows at them. Finally a strong wind rose. For six days they sailed with this tail wind, until they once again reached land. Later this was to be identified as the extreme southern point of Greenland, the same land which Nicolò had visited years before but at a point much farther north. They named it "Cape Trin," and the bay in which they anchored they called the "Bay of Trin."

That was in July. The weather was mild, the water teemed with fish and the air with sea birds. There was no human being in sight, but far in the distance they saw smoke rising above a mountain. Zichmi sent several men out to explore the land, and when they returned eight days later they reported that the smoke did not come from man-made fires but from the mountain itself. They had, however, seen some people along the way—small, shy creatures who fled into their caves as soon as they caught sight of the strangers.

When Zichmi heard the reports about the pure air, fertile soil and clean rivers, he decided to stay there with a group of volunteers to found a city. He sent the rest of the men back to Frisland under the command of Antonio. After first sailing twenty days due east, then five days southeast to Neome, and from there another three days westward, they finally reached their destination. Much to the joy, no doubt, of the friends and family they had left behind.[63]

At this point the story broke off. No one knew what eventually became of Antonio or of Zichmi's settlement on Greenland.

- – "But Mercator doesn't seem to doubt that the story is true. He must have found it in Ramusio's collection, because Santi and Rustene from Piero Quirino's travel reports are also on his map, and that's something he could only have gotten from that book."[64]

---

63   Zeno-Major 1873, p. 4-34.
64   Ramusio 2 1574, p. 206 recto - 211 verso (Ramusio 4 1983, p. 79-98).

Santi, the Island of the Saints, was an uninhabited rock mass where Piero Quirino, another Venetian who was carried off by the winds, had been shipwrecked in the year 1431.

The story went that he and his crew had managed to stay alive for the first nine days by eating the flesh of a stranded whale, and that they then lived on mussels and other shellfish until they were rescued by a few fishermen from the small neighboring island of Rustene. The rescue was in itself a kind of miracle. The sixteen-year-old son of one of the fishermen dreamt that two lost heifers had swum to this island, and he nagged his father and older brother about it for so long that they finally went with him to make a search. And there they found the castaways. They took them aboard their own ship and cared for them with great kindness.

Rustene reportedly had no more than twelve houses and about one hundred and twenty inhabitants. They lived mainly from fishing, and so excelled in piety and virtue that a visitor might have thought he had stumbled into Paradise. Lust and adultery were unknown there. Everyone—father, mother, grown sons and daughters, as well as guests—slept in the same room, naked as newborn babes. What is more, the master of the house would go off fishing with his sons at the crack of dawn, leaving the Italian visitors alone all day with the women. Their innocence was such that it never even occurred to them that anything improper might happen. These people were so at one with the Lord that when a family member or friend died they gave thanks and rejoiced in His will.[65]

Mercator had situated this island group high above North Cape, near the entrance to the Arctic Ocean, between Norway and the four polar islands of the *Inventio Fortunata*.[66] Taken together, the polar islands, Grocland and Huitsarc, the Zeno islands and the pair Santi and Rustene constituted a geographic innovation no less important—and certainly no less influential—than his projection based on increasing degrees of latitude.[67]

For people involved in seafaring and trade it must have seemed convincing, for everything was documented by travel reports. There was a climate of self-assurance, a sense of living in an era of progress, despite the charred gables in the streets around the Great Market, the ravaged countryside and the freebooters of one party or another roaming the seas. Ortelius was emphatic on this point:

- "That will pass. But what will remain is all the new knowledge we've gained, everything that's been discovered. With all due respect to Ptolemy, we realize now, since Columbus and Vespucci, how much he didn't know. That's why every eyewitness account should be taken more seriously than his map, even reports that were written centuries ago. In the Middle Ages, as they call them nowadays,[68] people weren't stupid, you know."[69]

---

65   Purchas 13 1906, p. 417-437.
66   Mercator 1569 (1961).
67   Van Ortroy 1926, p. 635; Dreyer-Eimbcke 1994, p. 146-150.
68   Jauß 1970, p. 25.
69   For Mercator's view on this matter see Durme 1959, e.g. letter nr. 7, p. 74-81; Houtte 1963, p. 7.

Between the discussions with Hooftman and his agent Jan van de Walle, Brunel went to Old Lombard Street to see Ortelius' "museum," as he himself called it.[70] There Brunel leafed through the *Theatrum* and had Mercator's world map unscrolled on his table again and again. The separately printed bird's-eye view of the polar region was especially fascinating to him (see ill. 39).

It showed everything: the four vast polar lands surrounded by a dark fringe of mountains and divided by the four streams. Here and there were comments in Latin taken from the *Inventio Fortunata*: "This is the best and healthiest island in the entire north"; "this stream has three mouths and is frozen over for approximately three months every year"; "here live four-foot tall Pygmies, who are related to the people on Greenland known as Skraelings"; "this stream has five mouths and is so narrow and rapid that it never freezes"; and, of course, on the island above the extreme west of the New Indies, also called America, "the ocean which penetrates between the islands with nineteen mouths forms four gulf streams, through which it flows continually northward, where it is sucked deep inside the earth. Precisely beneath the pole stands a rock measuring approximately thirty-three German miles in circumference." And there stood the rock itself, black and huge.

It was amazing. A wealth of new information and all so clearly presented. Mercator's world no longer bore the least resemblance to the old Ptolemaic maps. All that remained of those was the island Margaster, to the right of Greenland's northernmost cape.

Ortelius pointed to it and Brunel's face showed both recognition and surprise. Back in the fifteenth century, in the first Ptolemy editions, it had appeared under the name Margarester immediately northwest of the Norwegian coast.[71] When Greenland was moved eastward this island became its close neighbor, and it remained so when Greenland was later shifted back to the west. There it was, at the same latitude as the St. Thomas monastery, near the passage to the western Sucking Sea, through which any ship wishing to reach Grocland would have to sail.

- "But to get to the Strait of the Three Brothers you'd be better off sailing past Cape Trin on the southern coast of Greenland and then along Estotiland to the northwest."
- "Is that possible?"
- "Who can say? The storms there are more violent than anywhere else, and when it's not storming there's always the ice. Cabot never made it through. But Frobisher claims that on his first voyage he reached an open sea that stretched out to the west.[72] Once he gets back from his second voyage we'll know if it's as open as he thought."
- "In any case, though, the monopoly on that route is still in English hands, and they'll undoubtedly want to keep it that way."

---

70   Denucé 2 1913, p. 5.
71   See e.g., Nordenskiöld 1889 (1970), plate nr. 30 "Mare congelatum" (1467) and Ptolemy 1482 (1963), "Mare congelatum."
72   *State papers* 1862, p. 13-14, nr. 27.

39. Gerard Mercator, *The Northern Polar Region* (1569).
    Mercator combines all the information collected up to that point: we see here the four
    polar islands with the four streams between them; the black rock; a note about the Pyg-
    mies; Grocland, Greenland and the small islands of Santi and Rustene. On the basis of new
    calculations, however, the Magnetic Mountain, also in the form of a black rock, has been
    placed at the entrance to the Strait of Anian, between Asia and America.

- "True enough."
- "And the northeast passage?"

Ortelius did not believe it existed. Even if it could be proved that Burrough had managed to pass Vaygach.[73]

- "Oh, there's no doubt about that. I did it myself. It's not easy, but it can be done."[74]

But then there was still that peninsula stretching eighty degrees to the north. Impossible to get around it. And even if someone did manage to sail straight through all those ice floes and reefs and sandbanks, the journey would still be doomed by the great magnetic rock which Mercator had situated in the middle of the entrance to the Strait of Anian. There it stood, precisely mid-way between Asia and America, an exact copy of the black rock at the pole.[75]

- "But why?"
- "Why? Because the compass deviations indicate that there's a separate magnetic pole, at some distance from the North Pole. Mercator already realized that thirty years ago and managed to calculate its location."
- "How?"
- "A seaman from Dieppe—his name was François, if you want to know all the details—reported that the compass needle always points in the same direction when you're on the meridian that runs through the Cape Verde islands. Which means that the magnetic pole must be located at that longitude. Later he mentioned another location more to the northwest as a possible alternative, the meridian of the Azores.[76] Such a scientific mind he has. Prefers alternatives to false certainties…"
- "And all that means…"
- "Ah, yes, it means that whether you take the northwest or the northeast route, it will be virtually impossible in either case to enter the Strait of Anian. The compass would go crazy. No human being can navigate there, and we have nothing else to go by either—no maps, no reports, nothing."[77]
- "But is it true?"

Ortelius grinned:

- "Who can say? Mercator himself is pretty proud of it, in any case. Let me show you something."

---

73   Hakluyt 1 1598, p. 433; Tracy 1980, p. 11-13.
74   Hakluyt 1 1598, p. 511.
75   Mercator 1569 (1961).
76   Ortroy 1926, p. 648; Durme 1959, nr. 18, p. 32-34; Smet 1962, p. 80-83.
77   Hakluyt 1 1598, p. 444; Durme 1959, nr. 143, p. 158-159.

He opened a drawer and took out an engraving:

– "Look, this is the portrait that my good man Frans Hogenberg made of him three years ago" (see ill. 40).[78]

Brunel looked closely: there sat the man known as the princely mathematician and court cosmographer of the Duke of Clève, staring into the distance with a strange light in his eyes. In his right hand he held a pair of compasses, the point of which had been carefully placed on the magnetic pole of the globe in front of him. The words "polus magneticus" identified the spot.

– "Do you see anything unusual?"

40. *Gerard Mercator.*
    By Frans Hogenberg (1574). Unlike the rest of the picture, the globe appears in mirror image and in a position to show the polar islands, Greenland, North America, and the Magnetic Mountain.

78   Denucé 1 1912, p. 265.

- "What should I see?"
- "Look closely. It's all in mirror image. But in such a way that the globe shows everything this master is famous for—not only the polar islands and Greenland, but the northern part of America in its full breadth, as well as the Strait of Anian and the magnetic pole. Good old Frans did such a good job that at first glance you don't even notice that something's wrong."[79]

Brunel was no longer listening. His thoughts wandered back to Russia, to Lampas and farther east, into Siberia and up to the mouth of the Ob', where the sandbanks and ice floes were more treacherous and the Samoyeds more dangerous than anywhere else. Did Ortelius then, perhaps, talk to Brunel about the other possibility, the one mentioned already by Von Herberstein, of sailing up the Ob' into the interior? Both he and Mercator were, after all, familiar with Von Herberstein's book.[80]

In the course of that same year, 1577, Olivier Brunel returned to Russia in the company of Jan van de Walle. He had finally convinced Hooftman that a trade connection via Kola, set up in cooperation with the Stroganovs, would be so profitable that any objections which the English might raise would prove negligible. While it was true that Hooftman owed his wealth mainly to trade with England, the relations with merchants there had been so strained for the last several years that one more problem would make little difference.[81] Van de Walle established himself in Kola, and a short time later at the mouth of the Dvina. Before long ships were plying the route between Antwerp and the White Sea. In 1580 Hooftman recommended that the Antwerp city government set up a central storage and sales point for salt salmon. He had great expectations, for that product in particular.[82]

In the meantime Frobisher had returned from his second voyage. And from his third voyage. He still maintained that it was possible to sail through the Strait of Anian, but the gold which he brought back with him proved, after endless testing, to be worthless, and the "Company of Cathay" was declared bankrupt. Instead of being granted a noble title Frobisher was accused of mismanagement and fraud.[83] But this gave the Muscovy Company a new chance. On May 30, 1580 Arthur Pet and Charles Jackman set out with two ships to make yet another attempt at a northeast passage.[84]

As early as April of that year someone from England—possibly John Dee himself, who had written the instructions for the voyage—secretly informed Mercator of the plans. The information arrived too late for him to send Pet and Jackman his advice. But he set forth his view of the expedition at great length in a letter to Hakluyt. The route along the north coast was blocked by the Isthmus of Tabin, and farther along by the Magnetic Mountain. The rivers offered the only hope: they were broad and slow, mak-

---

79   Frans Hogenberg, Mercator. In Mercator 1595 (1963).
80   Henning 1906, p. 143 (Mercator); Ortelius 1570 (1964), p. 45 recto.
81   Smedt 1 1950, p. 295-297; Brulez 1959, p. 271 and 452-453; Wijnroks 1993, p. 46 and
      50-51.
82   Kernkamp 1903, p. 262-263; Wassenaer 8 1628, p. 90 verso - 91 recto; Denucé (1938), p. 14.
83   Cf. *State papers* 1862, especially nr. 142, p. 55-60; Wallis 1984, p. 461.
84   Hakluyt 1598, p. 433.

ing it easy even for large ships to travel inland. From the mouth of the Ob' to Peking, seat of the great khan, it could not be more than three hundred German miles.[85] Later, he secretly passed the information on to Ortelius.[86]

All this time Brunel was wandering through Russia, dreaming about the same possibilities. Years ago in Yaks Olgush he had, after all, heard talk of a river with a name similar to Ardock. The Ardock—Willem van Rubroeck had written about it centuries earlier, and Jenkinson had mentioned it in his report on the long journey he had made straight across Russia to Aghanistan and Persia for the purpose of meeting the caravans from the far east.[87] It had to be the same river, the great connecting route sailed by ships on their way to the west, with dark-skinned crews and large cargoes of precious goods—silk and aloes, musk and rhubarb—[88]and it had to be accessible via the Ob' and the Lake of Kittay.[89]

He probably had little difficulty convincing the Stroganovs, Anika's sons Semyon and Yakov and his grandsons Maxim Yakolevich and Nikita Grigorevich, that it was urgent to take matters into their own hands. Mercator and Ortelius had no idea of the dangers lurking along the banks of the Ob' and the Irtysh, which they saw simply as easily navigable rivers. In any case Kuchum, the khan who had united the Tartar tribes in that region, would have to be pacified. And the Stroganovs were the only people capable of getting this job done. Maxim had cultivated relations with a certain Yermak, leader of a small army of cossacks.[90] The right kind of ships—not too large and, most importantly, not too deep but nevertheless with ample cargo space—could best be built in the new settlement on the White Sea, where the archangel Michael would give them his special protection. Seamen would have to be brought in from Antwerp, as would goods attractive enough to catch the eye of the khan of all Tartars in far-off Peking and interest him in the prospect of trade…

85   Durme 1959, nr. 143, p. 157-159; Hakluyt 1 1598, p. 444-445; Tracy 1980, p. 16-17.
86   Ortelius 1887, nr. 99, p. 238-239; Durme 1959, nr. 148b, p. 162-163.
87   Purchas 12 1906, p. 13; Willan 1968, p. 56-57.
88   Purchas 12 1906, p. 25.
89   Henning 1906, p. 18-21; Hakluyt 1 1598, p. 512.
90   Fischer 1 1768, p. 186.

VI *The Northeast Passage*

It was such a good plan… Certain moments in the past seem to reshuffle the years around them, throwing the actual order of events into confusion. When Olivier Brunel came to Mercator with his proposal in February or early March of 1581, the latter had already formulated his opinion on the matter and sent it off to England half a year earlier—on July 28, 1580 to be exact:

> The voyage to Cathay by the east is doubtless very easy and short, and I have oftentimes marvelled that, being so happily begun, it hath been left off, and the course changed into the west, after that more than half of your voyage was discovered. For beyond the island of Vaygach and Novaya Zemlya there followeth presently a great bay, which on the left side is enclosed with the mighty promontory Tabin. Into the midst hereof there fall great rivers, which passing through the whole country of Russia, and being as I think navigable with great vessels into the heart of the continent, may be an easy means whereby to traffic for all manner of merchandise, and transport them out of Cathay… I think from the mouth of the mighty rivers Bautisus and Ob' to the chiefest seat of the great prince the khan there are not more than three hundred German miles…[1]

This same route had already been described in great detail by John Dee in the instructions which he had drawn up for the voyage of Pet and Jackman to Cathay. How tempting it is to assume that the merchant John Balakus from Arensberg on the Baltic island Ösel was confused about the western calendar and made an error of one year when writing the date. In that case Mercator would have had ample time to pass Brunel's ideas on to John Dee, who could then have incorporated them into his instructions…

Nonsense, of course. The instructions themselves made reference to Ortelius' map of 1570, which also showed a peninsula stretching far beyond the eightieth parallel. And everyone was familiar with Von Herberstein's account, already published in 1549, which described black people from Cathay floating down or sailing up the rivers which had to be so easily accessible from the Ob'. Besides, Mercator himself expressed his regret that he had heard about the plans too late to give any advice. Although, was it really too late? When he wrote to Ortelius in December of 1580 he let slip that by April of that year he already knew what was in the offing.[2]

---

1   Durme 1959, nr. 143, dd. July 28, 1580, p. 158-159; Hakluyt 1 1598, p. 444-445.
2   Ortelius 1887, nr. 99, p. 238-239; Durme 1959, nr. 148b, p. 162-163; Okhuizen 1992, p. 18-19. See also chapter I p. 16, chapter III p. 50-51 and chapter V p. 112.

But whoever borrowed the idea from whom, or whether each of them—John Dee, Gerard Mercator and Olivier Brunel—had come up with it independently, this attempt also came to nothing. The Year of our Lord 1581 was in every respect a dismal affair. And 1582 brought no improvement.

By the time Olivier Brunel returned to Antwerp with his commission from the Stroganovs and the backing of Mercator, everything there had changed. Gillis Hooftman had died in January around sixty years of age. Rumor had it that he had left one million guilders in gold; it was certain in any case that he had bequeathed no less than fifty thousand ducats to the city for assistance to the poor, with the stipulation that it be equally divided between Roman Catholics and Protestants.[3] It was a credit to his name and helped cement the peace between the religious factions which the Prince of Orange had proclaimed for a second time two years before, giving a new boost to trade. But it was not enough to turn the tide.

More and more Catholics were leaving the city; at the same time the stream of Calvinist refugees grew steadily larger as Alexander Farnese, Duke of Parma, slowly but surely began winning back one city after another for the Spanish king: Kortrijk, Breda and, most recently, Doornik. Reduced to poverty, they found shelter with fellow Protestants and, in some cases, simply lived on the street. The city seemed to be holding its breath. Rumors filled the air—Catholic masses would be completely forbidden, the Duke of Parma was about to begin a decisive campaign, the Italian and German merchants were considering a move to Cologne and the English to Middelburg. Then, on July 26, 1581, the States-General of the northern regions, which Antwerp had also joined, renounced their loyalty to their sovereign Prince Philip II.[4]

- – "That means war."
- – "It is war."
- – "True enough."
- – "But trade must go on."
- – "Yes, of course, the only question is where."

Trade did go on. In the north Jan van de Walle moved his office from Kola to what was known as the Podesyemsco mouth of the Dvina east of St. Nicholas, one of the four points at which this river emptied into the White Sea. There he built a house and several warehouses.[5]

Whether he managed this on his own or was financed by the heirs of Hooftman or by others—Gillis van Luffelt perhaps, or the company Simon van Salingen, which had been trading at Kola since the 1560's,[6] or Balthasar de Moucheron—more ambitious plans were out of the question as long as his position there was not stronger and it

---

3 Berens 1968, p. 70 and 74; Zweite 1980, p. 321.
4 Prims 8.1 1941, p. 156 and 165; Thijs 1990, p. 26-28; Groenveld-Leeuwenberg 1979, p. 110-113.
5 Cordt 1891, p. 248-249; Kernkamp 1909, p. 30; Wijnroks 1993, p. 50-51; Wassenaer 8 1625, p. 91 recto.
6 Jansma 1946, p. 347, 353 and 360; Linschoten 1914, p. 215, 220-222.

remained unclear just how favorably disposed Ivan IV was towards this infringement of the English monopoly.

- "And one other thing: before Jackman gets back no one will want to invest a cent in that sort of venture. I wouldn't myself, no matter how tempting it is."

They were very different people, Gillis Hooftman and Balthasar de Moucheron. Barely thirty years old, the latter was already director of one of the fastest growing trading companies in the city, although he did most of his business from Flushing, where the rebels had been firmly established for some time. He was a convinced Calvinist who dreamt of new worlds not only for the sake of profit, but especially to bring about the proclamation of God's word over the entire earth:

- "You know, Brunel, all that matters in the end is that people who are still worshipping the devil will come to know Christ and spread the honor of God."[7]
- "People like the Lapps or Samoyeds, and the Tartars."

De Moucheron blustered his reply:

- "Yes, yes, you're right, and someday we'll go there, I promise. But there are more heathens in the world, even right here in Antwerp. What do you think of our Ortelius, the way he so eagerly put all the fantasies of that fool Postel into his *Theatrum*?"
- "At least he didn't put Paradise up in the north."
- "Just wait. They still seem to be corresponding and I hear that Postel himself has now published a map of the polar region with everything on it: the holy land of Sveta Zemlia and Mount Stolp, which is supposed to be the pillar of the world.[8] Would you believe, he says it's Mount Zion of the Psalmist, 'the joy of the whole earth is Mount Zion, on the sides of the north, the city of the great King.'[9] Ha, ha, you have to be careful when you sail past Vaygach, you might get sucked right into heaven."
- "Or into hell."
- "Right. For the time being we'll have to be satisfied with Greenland, where the monks chant their prayers for the Skraelings like John the Baptist for the grasshoppers in the desert."

There was no alternative, if he wanted to achieve anything more than sailing year after year between Kola and Flushing or some other Dutch port.

Meanwhile in the east, the Cossack leader Yermak Timofeyevich had conquered the Tartar city of Sibir on the Irtysh. That was in 1581, two years after he and his army of about eight hundred men had crossed the Urals. The report of this victory, and especially the furs which accompanied it—twenty-four hundred sable, eight hundred black

---

7   De Stoppelaer 1901, p. 23-24; Schallenberg-van Huffel 1927, col. 884-885.
8   Ortelius 1887, nr. 81, p. 186-192; Destombes 1985, p. 366-368.
9   Psalm 48:2-3.

fox and two thousand beaver—created quite a stir in Moscow. The tsar had already sent reinforcements to consolidate the conquered territory.[10]

But money always had the final say on where the ships would sail. And one of the few people still able to finance an expedition was Balthasar de Moucheron. So in March of 1583 Olivier Brunel and Arent Meyer from Bergen in Norway made an agreement with the king of Denmark that they would attempt, at their own expense—that is, at De Moucheron's expense—to find the lost country of Greenland. In return they would be given compensation for their investments, a monopoly on the trade route to Greenland and, if they should decide to establish themselves in Bergen for the purpose of plying this route, six years exemption from taxes.

Shortly thereafter Brunel must have changed his home port from Antwerp to Enkhuizen.[11] The situation in the south was gradually becoming intolerable, even though De Moucheron still refused to entertain any thoughts of leaving the city on the Schelde.[12] It was probably from Enkhuizen that Brunel left on the voyage which took him first to Bergen, then along the Faeroe Islands in the direction of Frisland and Iceland, and from there on toward Greenland. To establish trade and to spread the one true Christian faith.

The most direct impetus for the Greenland plan might have been that De Moucheron, or Brunel himself, had gotten hold of age-old descriptions of that part of the world, including the necessary sailing instructions. They had been collected at the beginning of the century by the Archbishop of Trondheim, Erik Walkendorf, who had asked Christian II for free access to the sea route plus ten years tax exemption; that was only a little less than Christian's distant cousin Frederick spontaneously offered Brunel. But Walkendorf had fallen into disfavor with his plan. Like Olaus Magnus a few decades later, he had set out for Rome, stopping in Amsterdam along the way. There were even rumors that he had died in the Carthusian monastery just outside the Dutch city. Since then, copies of the old travel accounts kept circulating, as well as Danish, Latin and German translations.[13]

The most important of these descriptions was the one written in the second half of the fourteenth century by Ivar Bardsen, himself a native of Greenland and steward of the estates of the Bishop of Gardar on what was called the "East Bay."[14] Bardsen gave a very different picture of Greenland from that found in other writings. Instead of wasted, malnourished descendants of Normans who lived in huts made of whale ribs, twigs and moss, and who were easy prey for the rampaging Lapps and Skraelings,[15] he described—at least in Osterbygd—a fairly prosperous community.

He told of vast plains covered with green grass as far as the eye could see. And of a fjord, surrounded by sandbanks, where thousands of whales came at high tide only to strand there when the tide went out again. Farther to the east, on the side of the glaciers, stood large crosses constructed during the time of St. Olaus on the spot where his

---

10   Fisher 1943, p. 26-27.
11   Linschoten 1914, p. liv-lv; Jansma 1946, p. 348-350.
12   Groenveld-Leeuwenberg 1979, p. 112-113.
13   Burger 1928, p. 225-226, 236-237; Dreyer-Eimbcke 1994, p. 138.
14   Zeno-Major 1873, p. xv, 52-53; Burger 1928, p. 225-226 and 231.
15   See chapter V, p. 97.

drowned companions were buried. This was also the habitat of the dreaded white bear. But there were a few settlements near the grasslands as well: monasteries dedicated to St. Olaus and St. Augustine, and a convent of Benedictine nuns situated on a fjord full of small islands with hot water springs—boiling hot in the winter and lukewarm in the summer—which were used as healing baths. He wrote nothing about a Dominican monastery or about the Church of St. Thomas mentioned by Mercator. But a Holy Cross Church and a St. Nicholas Church and even a cathedral did appear in his work. And all those monasteries and churches owned fjords teeming with fish, as well as fertile grasslands and forests full of reindeer. Just off the coast there was even an island with eight large orchards. Exceptionally tasty apples grew on the lower slopes of the mountains, and on the plains the people raised grain of the highest quality. Besides Gardar he mentioned the following settlements by name: Ketilsfjord and Vatsdal, Dalr, Hvalsöe, Thjodhildestad, Dyrnaes, Loide and Brattelid.[16]

Not a trace of all this could be found on the maps of Mercator or Ortelius, or of anyone else, for that matter. But the information was so detailed—as could be expected coming from a steward—that there was no reason to doubt its reliability. The Zeno brothers might have given different names to the places, but on the most important points they reported similar findings: fertile ground, hot water springs, and a relatively mild climate, certainly in the southeast. The scientific explanation had already been given by Ziegler when he pointed out that land penetrated by the most bays and inlets would have to be the warmest and most fertile.[17]

The west side, Bardsen maintained, had once been equally prosperous, and as an episcopal see had even boasted a cathedral. But there the Pygmies, or Skraelings as he called them, had wreaked their worst, and none of the original inhabitants had survived. Bardsen himself had taken part in a relief expedition sent there by the Bishop of Gardar. But they found no one, neither Christians nor heathens, only some livestock roaming aimlessly through the countryside, horses, oxen, and sheep. They loaded as many as possible into their ships and returned to Osterbygd, twelve nautical miles down the coast, where the wild tribes had apparently not yet caused any trouble.

All this Ivar Bardsen, steward of Gardar, had put into writing, adding that the polar bears in Greenland had a red spot on their forehead and that the land abounded in silver, ivory and walrus pelts, as well as marble and tufa stone.[18] Others told of mountains of gold and silver, and pelts not only of walrus but of marten, sable and ermine as well.[19] Everything to make a merchant's heart beat faster. Of course the climate had worsened considerably since then.[20] But surely not everything described by Bardsen and Zeno could have disappeared completely? There was, in any case, ample reason to try to reestablish the connection, especially since stories were still circulating around the markets of Europe about the ivory and the walrus hides from Greenland, and since now and then shipments would arrive which, incredibly, seemed to have come from none

---

16   Zeno-Major 1873, p. 42-52; Burger 1928, p. 228-230.
17   Zieglerus-Krantzius 1583, p. 477; see also chapter V p. 96-97 and p. 104-106.
18   Zeno-Major 1873, p. 52-54; Burger 1928, p. 231.
19   Burger 1928, p. 233; Purchas 13 1906, p. 169.
20   Hennig 2 1950, p. 284.

other than that lost land.[21] The idea of establishing a way station for a possible north-west passage to Cathay was at most a secondary consideration—but Frobisher's failure left that monopoly open again as well…[22]

It was probably a clear, cold morning when Arent Meyer and Olivier Brunel, together with six other men,[23] left the green slopes and small red houses of the Norwegian coast behind them and set sail for Iceland. How they fared on their voyage is not difficult to imagine. Up to Iceland it must have been relatively easy. At most, on a windy night with the full moon shining, a sailor might have thought he saw Holler flying past on his fish bone; or, as they neared the Icelandic coast, the men might have scanned the horizon for tell-tale signs of smoke or crows. As the white ice field of the Vatnajokel appeared above the clouds, they steered a course along the coast, passing Westmann and Reykjanes, which according to Ortelius was called Hekelfort.

- "Hecklefield, you mean, where the devil brings the soul of the Bishop of Bremen."

They went as far as Snaefjelsnes on the west coast, where the crossing to Greenland was supposed to be the shortest.

The sailing instructions were clear enough. Heading west for one day and one night would bring them to the Gunnbjorn rocks. Long ago this had been the most common route, but the climate had turned so much colder in the meantime that ice from the north had gathered in a large area around the rocks, forcing ships to make a detour to the south. Once past this obstacle they would have one more day and night of sailing in a northwest direction before reaching Hvarf, a mountain or hill on the coast of Greenland. One day past Hvarf lay Huitsarc, and between these two landmarks was the Isthmus of Herjulfnaes, with the good harbor of Sandhavn nearby.[24]

There were uncertainties, however. Olaus Magnus, for example, had maintained that Huitsarc was the same as the rocks of Gunnbjorn, and that was how it appeared on the maps of Mercator and Ortelius, exactly halfway between Iceland and Greenland.[25] Johannes Ruysch's map, on the other hand, reported that a rocky island on this spot had completely burned up in 1456, indicating one of the volcanic eruptions common to this area.[26] In any case there was a point from which you could see both the Snaefjelsjokel on Iceland and the mountains of Greenland, almost everyone agreed on that.[27] But it was also generally known that from the depths of the northern seas—the Troll Troughs as they called them in Norwegian—ice came floating down in such quantities, bringing with it so much fog and mist, that the area between Iceland and Greenland was one immense wasteland of icebergs and gray desolation.

---

21 Lucas 1937, p. 178-179.
22 Jansma 1946, p. 349.
23 Cf. Jansma 1946, p. 361.
24 Zeno-Major 1874, p. 39-42; Burger 1920, p. 227-228; cf. Hacquebord 1983, p. 45-48.
25 See chapter II, p. 36-37, ill. 12, and V, p. 90, ill. 32 and p. 99.
26 Nordenskiöld 1889 (1970), plate nr. 32; Hennig 2 1950, p. 191-193.
27 Burger 1928, p. 232; Hennig 2 1950, p. 190-193.

They were probably not so much surprised as simply afraid when they found neither the Gunnbjorn Rocks nor the pack ice which was supposed to indicate that the
rocks were nearby. Afraid of ending up in the slowly solidifying mass known as the sea
lung or the Liver Sea, or—worse still—in the Sucking Sea. Perhaps, while drifting
blindly in a suffocating mist, they came upon land, and in keeping with the stern advice
of the sailing instructions sent out just two men to scout the area.[28] They would surely
have returned in short order, with nothing to report. Perhaps they never knew whether
their destination was nearby or still a long way off.

Did Brunel's relations with his crew then deteriorate to to the point that they—
Jochem and Andries Meker, Jacob Timmerman, Pouwel Geerkens and Otto Meyeck,
all Germans, and the Norwegian Dirck Claeszoon—left him in the lurch with his ship
and cargo in the autumn of that same year? This happened on the return voyage to
Enkhuizen, when they had already passed the island of Texel, near the town of Wierin-
gen. Because, they insisted, the ship was threatened by ice floes. As if they had not
encountered ice a hundred times more threatening up in the north, those scoundrels.
But he would get his revenge.

That winter, at home with Suzanna in Enkhuizen, Brunel vented his rage to anyone
who would listen—seamen and merchants, in the pub and on the street. Until the six
men jointly took him to court on charges of slander and demanded that he pay dam-
ages, with the result that this man, in whom some of the greatest merchants in the
world had placed their trust, now found himself scrambling for guarantors in the back-
waters of a provincial Dutch town.[29]

But the end of the winter brought news which changed everything: Anthony
Marsh of the Muscovy Company had received a letter from Russia informing him that
an English ship had capsized near the mouth of the Ob' and that the crew had been
murdered there by the Samoyeds.[30]

So Jackman, too, must have managed to navigate the small passage along Vaygach.
That he lost his life in the process was sad, of course, but that was simply one of the
risks of being a merchant. Brunel was willing to bet that the man had been unable to
speak a word of Russian or Tartar, to say nothing of Samoyed. He, Brunel, would never
end up like that. Meanwhile, news also arrived about the fabulous numbers of hides
and furs which Yermak had sent to the tsar. And that was not all: the tsar himself had
founded a settlement, New Kholmogory, six miles upstream on the Dvina near the St.
Michael monastery, for the purpose of expanding trade with the west along this route,
now that he had lost the Baltic ports of Narva and Novgorod to Sweden. De
Moucheron, who up to that point had conducted his trade mainly via Narva, was now
finally prepared to focus his attention on the White Sea. And beyond. People were even
saying that he had approached the Prince of Orange about the possibility of exploring
the northern passage and that the prince had expressed great interest, even though he
saw no possibility of the government participating in this sort of undertaking.[31] But
there were private parties willing to give it a try.

---

28   Burger 1928, p. 233.
29   Jansma 1949, p. 349-350 and 361.
30   Armstrong 1984, p. 429.
31   Jansma 1946, p. 347-348; Wassenaer 8 1625, p. 91 recto; cf. Linschoten 1914, p. liv-lviii.

A ship was readied and filled with merchandise. Arent Meyer invested a good part of his money in it; for the rest it was financed by a syndicate of Antwerp merchants led by De Moucheron. At last, on a spring day in 1584, Brunel set sail from the Enkhuizen harbor. He stopped in Kola, of course, and in New Kholmogory (Archangel, as people were beginning to call it) where a fort was under construction as well as numerous houses, two inns, warehouses, a weighing station and an office for the collection of tolls.[32]

The town was abuzz with activity. The clear sound of hammers echoed through the air, ships rocked at anchor in the harbor, carts and sleighs moved back and forth along the waterfront. Everything seemed to indicate that this port, and not St. Nicholas, held the future of trade with Russia—even though people were worried, for Ivan the Terrible had died on March 18 and no one knew what policy his son and successor, Feodor Ivanovich, would pursue on such issues as the presence of the English.[33] Or of the Danes, for that matter, who had sent battleships as far as Podesyemsco in their attempt to enforce the payment of tolls to their king.[34] Perhaps it was there in Archangel, in one of the tsar's new inns, that Brunel spent the winter, close to the old Kholmogory where he had been taken prisoner by the Russians twenty years earlier. But he may also have stayed at the Podesyemsco mouth where his old friend Jan van de Walle still had his office and warehouses.[35]

In any case he made an attempt both in 1584 and 1585 to sail past Vaygach. That must have been on the north side of the island, along the coast of Novaya Zemlya. There, on the southern tip of the "holy island," he found a harbor which the Russians called Costins Serch, but no passage and no people with whom to trade (see ill. 41).[36] And of the mountain Sveta Gemla, which was said to reach up to heaven with its peak gleaming in continual sunlight, he found no trace whatsoever, even though the skies were clear and drifting ice was visible all the way to the horizon.[37] The land was low and muddy. And empty, except for the eternally screeching birds and the polar bears which kept turning up between ice floes at the most unexpected moments.

Brunel could not have guessed that in August of 1584 Yermak Timofeyevich had already drowned in the Irtysh after being attacked by the united Tartar hordes under the command of Khan Kuchum. For two years Yermak and his cossacks had plundered their way through Tartar territory. Then, however, the resistance struck back from all sides. With just a handful of men Yermak managed to fight his way back to the river. But as he swam toward the boats the weight of his chain mail—given to him by the tsar in appreciation for all the conquests made in his name—dragged him down into the depths.[38]

But Olivier Brunel was first of all a merchant, and when the second attempt at a passage also failed he decided to go to the mouth of the Pitsane or the Pechora on the northern coast of Russia. He must have had his reasons for not traveling farther west to Lampas, where Russians, Tartars, and Samoyeds came together twice every year to

32   Wassenaer 8 1625, p. 91 verso.
33   Willan 1968, p. 165.
34   Wassenaer 8 1625, p. 91 recto.
35   Wassenaer 8 1625, p. 91 recto.
36   Waghenaer 1592, p. 104 and 204; Jansma 1946, p. 351.
37   See chapter IV, p. 82.
38   Lengyel 1949, p. 39; Fischer 1 1768, p. 245.

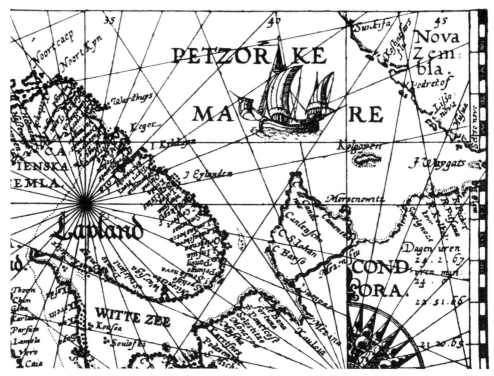

41. Lucas Janszoon Waghenaer, *The Arctic Ocean between Lapland and Novaya Zemlya* (1592).
Shown here are places which Brunel must have visited: New Kholmogory, Costins Serch on Novaya Zemlya, and the rivers Pechora and Pitsane.

trade their goods; or to the Colcolcova River, which flows between the Pechora and Lampas, and where traders from St. Nicholas and Kholmogory took on cargoes of pelts and rock crystal. Perhaps he hoped to outwit the competing Russians, English, and Danes by trading at a more eastern location, where everything would be cheaper because no other merchants came out that far. He did in fact manage to make contact with the Samoyeds there; they approached the river bank in their sleighs with great caution, ready to race off again at a moment's notice. With gestures and guttural sounds Brunel won their confidence; and in the end, squatting on the muddy ground and chewing on a piece of rancid reindeer fat, he came to an agreement with their chief about the number of hides and pelts which they would set out for him at some point farther upstream.

He transferred his goods to the longboat, and with a few men started rowing in the direction of the pick-up point. Suddenly, in the middle of that slow-moving river, they were caught in a whirlpool; scraping along a sandbank, the boat capsized and everyone in it drowned.[39]

---

39   Waghenaer 1592, p. 101 and 104; Hakluyt 1 1598, p. 284; Jansma 1946, p. 351-352; Horensma 1985, p. 126.

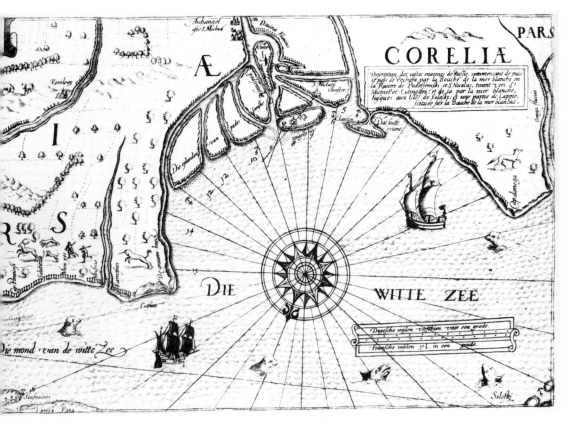

42. Lucas Janszoon Waghenaer, *The Northern Coast of Russia* (1592).
 The various trading centers at the Podesyemsco mouth of the Dvina are indicated here:
 St. Nicholas, where De Moucheron established himself; the English island; and New
 Kholmogory, where Van de Walle moved his trading post.

On August 17 of that same year, 1585, the representatives of besieged Antwerp, among them Balthasar de Moucheron, signed the document surrendering the city to the Duke of Parma. This finalized the division between the southern—Spanish, Catholic—Netherlands and the Protestant north. Everyone whose beliefs were shaped by the Reformation, by this time more than half of the population, left the city.[40] De Moucheron settled in Middelburg, where his father had resided for years and where he still had many contacts.[41] It was from there, three years later, that he permanently moved his office of Russian trade to the White Sea.

Feodor, the new tsar of all Russians, had decided to respond negatively to the English requests for a renewal of their monopoly. Van de Walle, who had already moved his trading post from the Podesyemsco mouth to Archangel in 1586, was making his influence felt (see ill. 42).[42] He himself spent most of his time in Moscow, gradually assuming

---

40   Thijs 1990, p. 10 and 38.
41   Schallenberg-van Huffel 1927, col. 885.
42   Wassenaer 8 1625, p. 91 verso.

the role of representative for all Dutch merchants. He was generally esteemed and, most importantly, a favorite of the tsar, whose needs for western luxuries he was always able to supply. In vain England's Queen Elizabeth protested against his presence. And when English ships finally tried to cut off access to the Dvina, Feodor sent an angry letter stating that he was not about to refuse entry to fifty or possibly even one hundred merchant vessels for the sake of six, or at most ten ships from England.[43]

But regardless of how many merchants accepted Van de Walle as their spokesman, De Moucheron, when dispatching his first ship to the White Sea under the command of his younger brother Melchior, sent it to St. Nicholas rather than to Archangel.[44] History repeated itself: while Melchior worked at expanding his trading post, his cousin and employee François de la Dale was arrested by the Russians. But this time it was not the English who were responsible but his own compatriot Van de Walle.[45]

How quickly fortunes changed! While De la Dale was learning Russian as a prisoner in Moscow, Van de Walle's business took a downhill course. Was it because trade with Antwerp had ground to a halt and his contacts had disappeared? Hooftman's sons had fled to Bremen,[46] others had moved to England or the northern Netherlands. The fact that he no longer had an established company backing him was beginning to take its toll. In 1589 there were already rumors of bankruptcy, and in 1591 it was a fact: Van de Walle—Beloborod, the venerable white-bearded old man, as the Russians called him[47]—was finished. Even the English saw new opportunities unfolding.[48] Not long after that De la Dale returned to the Netherlands.

– "François! Thank God! So the missive from the gentlemen of the States-General did help after all."[49]

For all practical purposes, the decision about Dutch involvement in the northern sea trade was made the moment that François de la Dale stepped into De Moucheron's house on Long North Street in Middelburg sometime in 1592.[50] That evening the two men sat for hours at the table in the spacious sitting room. Again maps were unrolled and Ortelius' atlas was opened. Besides learning Russian, De la Dale had also acquired other kinds of knowledge in Moscow, about Vaygach, for example, and about the coast of Russia and Tartary beyond the river Ob'.[51]

Around the same time Jan Huyghen van Linschoten returned to Enkhuizen after thirteen years of service with the Portuguese in the East Indies and the Azores. There he heard about Brunel from the mapmaker Lucas Janszoon Waghenaer.[52] Contacts

43   Cordt 1891, p. 248-250; Linschoten 1914, p. lxii-lxiii.
44   Kernkamp 1909, p. 49; Bartelds 1927, col. 889; Wijnroks 1993, p. 51-52.
45   *Resolutieën der Staten-Generaal* 7 1923, p. 392 and 8 1925, p. 498.
46   Berens 1968, p. 78-79.
47   Cordt 1891, p. 249.
48   Willan 1968, p. 188, 193, 246 and 251.
49   *Resolutieën der Staten-Generaal* 7 1923, p. 392.
50   Schallenberg-van Huffel 1927, col. 887.
51   Linschoten 1914, p. 28.
52   Linschoten 1914, p. xxv; Waghenaer 1592, p. 101, 104 and 204.

were made. De Moucheron spoke with the treasury secretary of Zeeland, Jacob Valcke; Valcke wrote to his colleague François Maelson, the municipal secretary of Enkhuizen; Maelson approached Linschoten. The admiralties of Zeeland and West Friesland, the state prosecutor and de facto leader of the Union, Johan van Oldenbarnevelt, and—following in the footsteps of his father—Prince Maurice in his function of admiral general, all showed interest. A first meeting was held in The Hague on December 28, 1593.[53]

- – "Make it very clear that we'll have to settle on a route around the south of Vaygach, then on past the Ob', following the coast of Tartary all the way."
- – "You're sure about that, François?"
- – "All the reports I heard in Moscow point in that direction."
- – "Not inland, then, via the Ob'?"
- – "No, no."

De la Dale was insistent. This, after all, was what was new about their plan compared to the previous attempts of Pet and Jackman, and of Brunel: their route would take them past Cape Tabin along the north coast all the way to China and Cathay. The idea, originally Sebastian Cabot's, had, in fact, served as the basis for the sailing instructions used by Willoughby, Burrough and Chancellor, and was now being championed by De la Dale in the face of all the more recent theories.[54]

During all these years the ideas which had once so inspired the circle around Plantijn lived on in Antwerp, where a strict Catholicism once again prevailed. The leading men of the group were now old or dead. Goropius Becanus, who had already left the city in 1570, died in 1572, Postel in 1581. Arias Montanus had been living in Spain ever since he was called back there in 1575, although he still corresponded with Plantijn, and since 1585 with increasing frequency, about the mystical prophecies of Hiël, the Apocalypse and the visions of Ezekiel.[55]

Traces of their scholarship could be found on the maps and in the atlases still being produced in large numbers in the city. Ortelius, for example, cited Becanus on the subject of the northern tribes: they were all Celts or Cimbri and spoke German; even the name of Europe could be traced back to the Germanic "E," meaning "legal marriage," plus "Ur" ("outstanding") plus "Hop" ("hope")—because it was the European and not the Arabic church that was the bride of Christ.[56]

But the man most admired by Ortelius was Postel. Up until two years before the latter's death, the two men had corresponded about the information which Ortelius had taken over from him for his map of Tartary.[57] Postel had called Ortelius' *Theatrum* the most important book since the Bible. He had explained how both of their names contained hidden forms of the Hebrew word for "morning dew," the sign of the living

---

53 Stoppelaar 1901, p. 94-95; Linschoten 1914, p. 27-28.
54 See chapter II, p. 44.
55 Brouwer 1953, p. 270 and 272; Rekers 1961, p. 30, 34-37 and 164-172.
56 Becanus 1569, p. 1045; Ortelius 1595, "Europa"; see also chapter IV, p. 72-73.
57 See chapter IV, p. 80-81, ill. 28.

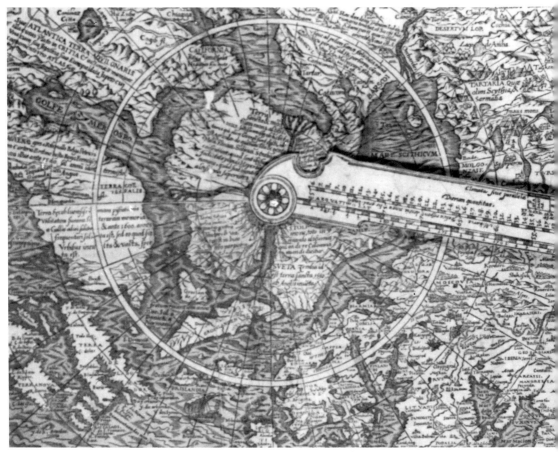

43. Guillaume Postel, *World Map in Polar Projection* (1578).
Despite the poor quality of the illustration it is clear that Postel has adopted Mercator's
polar projection. He places Stolp Mountain, the "pillar of the world," directly on the
North Pole, where he thought paradise should be.

Christ. And he had again written about the ten tribes of Israel and about his own newly
published map of the polar region, which showed everything in detail (see ill. 43).[58]

And indeed, this map, based on a polar projection borrowed from Mercator, offered
a clear picture of how it all fit together: the holy Hyperboreans, the land of Sveta Zemlya
and Mount Stolp, the pillar of the world. The Hyperborean Mountains had moved from
their traditional location in northern Russia up to the polar islands.[59] Since the word
Hyperborean was made up of "Eber," which in the language of Adam meant "wing,"
and "Reah," "long," it was clear that the highest mountain would be found in this range,
at the source of the most wind.[60] So these mountains had to be situated farther north than

---

58   Ortelius 1887, nr. 81, p. 186-192; Destombes 1985, p. 366.
59   Destombes 1985, p. 368. See also chapter III, p. 51.
60   Secret 1985, p. 305.

126

scholars had previously assumed. The reports about journeys made by happy inhabitants of the polar regions to the Greek island of Delos could not be used as a counterargument, for the sea between their homeland and the north of Europe and Asia froze over in the winter, allowing them to cross easily whenever they wished to bring their gifts to Apollo.

Although the map showed nothing called Paradise, it did mention holy people and a holy land as well as Stolp—Postel had found the name for this mountain in Von Herberstein[61]—and especially the pole as the happiest spot on earth. In times long past the ten lost tribes of Israel had tried to migrate there after being driven out of the northeast of Scythia. It was still reachable, Postel maintained, by way of the Hyperborean fields.[62] As he had explained to Ortelius, there were Scythians living up in the far northeast near Mount Tabor, descendants of Seth, who with their simple life close to nature were doing penance for the sins of Adam.[63]

- "Are they Gog and Magog, then, the tribes that Marco Polo believed to be the same as the Ung and the Mungul? Mercator put them on his world map, too."[64]
- "Who knows…"

Ortelius may not have believed all of this, but he did include a reference to Postel's map in the very next edition of his *Theatrum*. Around the same time the information on the map also appeared on a globe made in Antwerp.[65] And in 1593 the heirs of Ortelius' competitor, Cornelis de Jode, published a map with Mount Stolp situated exactly on the North Pole, just as it was on Postel's map.

- "And on that map they connect the peninsula that Ortelius already showed stretching northward directly beyond the Ob'—it may or may not be Tabin—to the polar island that lies to the north of it, which means that the sea beyond Vaygach is bounded by land" (see ill. 44).
- "That's because they didn't understand Postel's map. The gray spot they took to be land is only the ice that he claims the Hyperboreans cross over in the winter to reach the mainland.[66] He needed it that way if he was ever going to get his Jewish tribes back across the polar sea and on their way to the Holy Land to greet the Messiah at the end of time. If they weren't the hallucinations of a madman it would be blasphemy, for sure."
- "But you can find that connection between the polar islands and Europe on the oldest Ptolemy editions, too, the German ones published in the last century. And come to think of it, Ruysch has something of the sort on his map as well."[67]
- "Well, Johannes Ruysch…"
- "And Mercator. Did you know that the great Mercator once also made a world

61   Herberstein 1557, p. 90 recto.
62   Secret 1961, p. 360-361.
63   Ortelius 1887, nr. 81, p. 188-191; Secret 1981, p. 116.
64   Mercator 1569 (1961), leaf 12; see chapter III, p. 49.
65   Destombes 1985, p. 370.
66   Nordenskiöld 1889 (1970), nr. 48; Destombes 1970, p. 88-93.
67   See chapter II, p. 36-37, ill. 12 and p. 42.

map that shows the arctic continent joined to Russia just beyond the White Sea?[68] That's much too far west, of course, but the idea that the Kara Sea, or as some call it, the Scythian Sea, is an inland body of water does seem likely."

This was the view of the Amsterdam Protestant minister Plancius, and that lay at the heart of a very big problem.

44. Cornelis de Jode, *World Map in Polar Projection* (1592).
De Jode takes over Stolp Mountain from Postel. He also joins the Isthmus of Tabin with one of the polar islands, thus ruling out the possibility of a northeast passage.

---

68   Nordenskiöld 1889 (1970), nr. 43.

Ever since the December 1593 meeting in The Hague, which was also attended by the mayor of Amsterdam, Reinier Cant, the Amsterdam contingent had been making things difficult.[69] The person responsible for this was Plancius, who had also fled the southern Netherlands and, after accepting a call to Amsterdam in 1585, had built up a considerable reputation among the Amsterdam merchants as a navigation expert.[70] The man had enough contacts to make his authority credible. There was a certain Willem Barents, a skipper who had gotten hold of Ivar Bardsen's description of Greenland and translated it into Dutch.[71] And Mathijs Syvertszoon Lakeman, who claimed to have developed a new method for accurately determining longitude at sea; he had recently submitted an application for a patent to the States-General. Restless types, no doubt, more interested in adventure than in trade, and obsessed with a strange drive to seek out the farthest corners of the world. Plancius himself appeared to be at work making maps together with Mathijs Syvertszoon, using Mercator's projection with degrees of increasing size—the type of map which most helmsmen found far too complicated to use.[72]

- – "What route did you have in mind?"
- – "A more northern one, along the upper coast of Novaya Zemlya, or maybe straight across the pole" (see ill. 45).[73]
- – "Over land?"
- – "Who says there's land up there? Even Mercator's polar islands are based on nothing more than the obscure report of some medieval monk. The English found only a few scattered islands when they explored the area. Robert Thorne already recommended the polar route to the English king back in 1513. He believed that the greatest danger would be found within a radius of one and a half miles from the pole, but once you got past that and started going east you would soon get to Tartary, and from there it would be clear sailing to China.[74] Quite recently William Bourne made the same point: if there is no land up there that would be the best route. There can't be that many ice floes, with the sun on the horizon all summer long, with nothing but salt water, and no land. You know, of course, it's always near land, around rivers and bays, that you get ice formation, not out on the open sea."[75]

De Moucheron was not convinced. He was annoyed by the meddlesome behavior of the Amsterdam delegation. Had the initiative not come from him? Had he not supplied the necessary expertise? Was he not the one who was willing to underwrite no less than a quarter of all the costs?

69   Stoppelaar 1901, p. 94-98.
70   Veer 2 1917, p. v-xix; Burger 1915, p. 318-325.
71   Burger 1928, p. 225-239.
72   Wieder 1 1925, p. 40; Keuning 1946, p. 86-90.
73   Burger 1915, p. 323-325; cf. also Burger 1930, p. 63.
74   Burger 1915, p. 267; Wieder 1 1925, p. 38-39; Keuning 1946, p. 110-111; cf. also chapter II, p. 42.
75   Bourne 1599, p. 53 verso-54 recto; cf. Linschoten 1914, p. 29 and Veer 2 1917, p. xx.

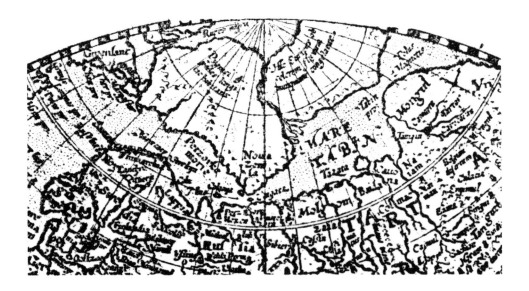

45. Petrus Plancius, *The Northern Polar Regions* (1590 and 1594 respectively).
     On the map of 1590 Novaya Zemlya is still part of the polar islands and the only possible
     passage is the one along Vaygach. On the map of 1594 Novaya Zemlya appears as an
     island, and the passage around the north of it is not only possible but also much broader
     than the one past Vaygach.

–   "Ivory-tower scholars, completely moonstruck about the North Pole. Whether
    they expect to find Paradise there or open water, it's all equally crazy. Speculation
    is a poor guide to action, my lad. You know, don't you, that the sea above Tar-
    tary is supposed to be so broad that you can sail through it all the way to
    Cathay?"

- "Yes, uncle. The scholar Paulus Jovius said so himself, and he was quoting merchants who had traveled there."[76]
- "Merchants, that's more like it. I want you to understand that we're sailing along the coast, no matter what the Amsterdammers are planning to do."
- "Yes, uncle."
- "And that you're coming along as an interpreter and clerk."

His plan, as submitted to the meeting in The Hague, was simple enough. The first voyage would be exploratory in nature and take place in deepest secrecy; no ports would be visited along the way. The Danes and the Russians would certainly make problems if they found out about it, and he already had his share of conflicts with them about tolls, trading rights, and monopolies.[77] Most important was that they explore the island Colgovia, or as the Russians called it, Kolguyev, which the Enkhuizen cartographer Lucas Janszoon Waghenaer placed about thirty-five miles west of Vaygach,[78] to see if it might be a suitable place for transferring cargoes. Since the passage was navigable for at most two months a year, it would be most efficient for the ships coming from China to unload their goods there and return immediately. Another advantage would be that the ships responsible for transport from there to the Netherlands would have to be at sea no more than four months at a time. An agricultural expert would have to accompany the expedition to determine whether the land was fertile enough for farming, and a military expert to decide on the best method of fortifying the island. Once that was all clear and the passage itself had been explored, they would return home. The crew would simply be told, sadly, that their mission had failed, that the distances were all too great, or something of that sort.[79]

The Amsterdam delegation, however, could not be swayed from the ideas put forward by their minister. And in the end three ships and a fishing vessel set sail from Texel in June 1594: the Swan, a ship equipped by de Moucheron, Valcke and the admiralty of Zeeland, with Cornelis Nay serving as captain and François de la Dale as merchant or clerk; the Mercury from Enkhuizen, equipped by Maelson and the admiralty of West Friesland, under the command of Brandt Tetgales as captain and with Jan Huyghen van Linschoten serving as merchant; and one more ship plus a fishing vessel, equipped by the merchants and admiralty of Amsterdam, under the command of Willem Barents, friend and confidante of Plancius.[80] The Swan and the Mercury would follow De Moucheron's plan and attempt a passage along Vaygach, but the Amsterdam ships would chart a more northern course from North Cape around the top of Novaya Zemlya.[81]

The weather was cold and damp and the sky dark with a stiff wind blowing from the southwest. Past North Cape fog closed in, allowing them only rare glimpses of land, even though they held a course no more than two miles from the coast. Near Kildin, an island north of Kola, the two Amsterdam vessels went their own way. As François de la

---

76   Linschoten 1914, p. 234-235; see also chapter II, p. 44.
77   Kernkamp 1909, p. 47-50; *Resolutieën der Staten-Generaal* 8 1925, p. 498.
78   Waghenaer 1592, p. 103.
79   Veer 2 1917, p. 183-186; Linschoten 1914, p. lxvii-lxix.
80   Linschoten 1914, p. 34, note 1.
81   Linschoten 1914, p. lxvi.

Dale watched them sail off, his uncle's words came back to him: "…strange characters, more interested in adventure than in trade."

The sky was clear that day and the sea calm. Gulls and loons cried around the ship, and a little farther off schools of whales frolicked in the water. They passed Kolguyev.

- "Weren't we supposed to explore that island?"
- "Later, later. First we have to find out for sure if a passage is possible."

Then, about twenty miles farther along, it all started happening. De la Dale, standing on deck, gasped at what he saw. At first it seemed to be only more fog. But it was ice. Left and right it stretched as far as the eye could see, with mist hovering over it in a layer so thick that it looked like land.

Upon coming closer they saw that it was not a solid mass as it had first appeared, but countless floes three or four fathoms thick protruding out of the water, washing up over each other, and floating apart again. They sailed into it a mile or so, and it was all the same: one endless shifting mass, with here and there black holes of water and thick trails of mist, and everywhere—in the water and on the ice—splashing and sliding and leaping from one floe to another, were seals.

There was no way through. For two days they steered south around the ice until they reached the Russian coast again near Candenoes. From there they set a new course eastward. Icebergs, some of them as large as the ships themselves, floated toward them, and before they knew it they were surrounded by towering masses of what looked like white rock, complete with cliffs and caverns with water flowing in and out. Before long the fog closed in again, as the ice slowly but steadily began to encircle the ship. All this time an ominous blood-red sun was hanging low on the horizon, and a strange light kept flashing in the sky, first in one place, then another—it was so disorienting that they soon lost all sense of how far they had come.

Sixteen days they continued along the Russian coast, caught between the ice and the land, hailing lodyas along the way to inquire about their position, and about Vaygach. De la Dale used his best Russian: was it true that a much warmer sea lay beyond Vaygach, and that the currents always came from there, even though the ice kept floating towards Novaya Zemlya? Was it true that the strait between Vaygach and the mainland was strewn with rocks? And was it true that so many walruses and sea horses made their home there that they alone would make a passage all but impossible?

But then came a day when all the ice suddenly disappeared. They sailed on and in three days reached Vaygach.

It was green there, without a single tree, of course, but green and flat, with meadows full of flowers. Only on the side facing the open sea were there rocks and reefs; these were interspersed with pebble or black sand beaches piled high with driftwood, branches and entire uprooted trees which must have been carried there by unusually powerful currents. From the east, no doubt, for they had encountered no sign of western currents of such force at any point in their voyage. Here and there stood tall crosses erected by Russian fishermen as beacons.

On the far southwest corner of the island they discovered three to four hundred wooden statues leaning against boulders or knolls, all facing eastward. Around them lay countless sets of antlers, apparently offerings made to these idols. Some of the carvings were half rotted away, others seemed new. There were men, women, in some cases a man and a woman together as one statue, and children; also poles with four or five and sometimes as many as seven or eight faces arranged vertically, as if they belonged to one family. It could not have been a burial ground, for there were no graves. More likely it was a kind of shrine, or place of pilgrimage. A wooden frame resembling a litter was lying there as well, as if the images were regularly carried in processions.

No human beings lived there. Only later, across the strait on the mainland, did they encounter any natives. First a hostile group of about thirty, all in sleighs pulled by two or three reindeer. With a rain of arrows they chased the explorers back to their ships. Eventually, however, Jan Huyghen managed to strike a more friendly tone. That was during their second attempt to sail through the Strait of Vaygach, which they renamed Nassau Strait.

The first time they had been driven back about one and a half miles by a storm and currents, and by the ice floes sweeping along with them. Some of the crew started grumbling: they had said all along that it was impossible, that when Brunel had tried it years before he had found the strait frozen over in midsummer, and there was no reason to believe that things would be different now.[82] But this time they succeeded (see ill. 46). Carefully steering a middle course, they sailed through the strait from Idol Point to Cross Point, as a large crowd gathered to watch from the mainland. Beyond Cross Point the strait curved around. The water turned salty and took on a clear shade of blue—there was no doubt about it, they were near open sea. At Dispute Point, named after the disagreement about whether the strait ended there, they erected a marker and crossed over to the other side. There they finally managed to strike up a conversation with the natives, although they kept their bows and arrows clutched in their hands and had their sleighs ready for a quick escape at the first sign of danger.

They were small ungainly people, dark, with pitch black hair hanging down over their eyes. The men had no beards; it appeared that they plucked out the hairs one by one. Their clothes were made of animal skins, with the fur or hair on the outside; caps and gloves were sewn onto their jackets. Some wore an additional colorful hat, similar to the kind worn by the women of Emden in Friesland. According to Jan Huyghen their bows and arrows resembled those used by the Persians; and their sleighs, which looked like wagons with the railing and bar construction on their high, open sides, were very different from those used by the Lapps in Kildin. They said that farther along there was a large sea, also that the strait would be ice-free in ten to twelve days, after which there would be six full weeks without frost.

With a great deal of shouting and waving and bowing Linschoten and his group finally said their farewells and sailed on. On a small island at the extreme eastern corner of the strait they placed a barrel on top of a pole as a beacon; from then on that spot was known as Barrel Point. From there they sailed into the open Tartar or Scythian Sea, which proved to be eighty fathoms deep, with high waves and water the color of azure, like all the oceans in the world, which meant that it almost certainly extended as far as China and Japan. So they sailed on, occasionally passing gigantic icebergs and giving names to all the islands and bays along the way: Maelson's Island, Staten Island, Cape Linschoten…

The water and land were teeming with life: walruses, whales, polar bears. At one point the men tried to kill a walrus, for the ivory in those tusks, they knew, was no less

82   Linschoten 1914, p. 229.

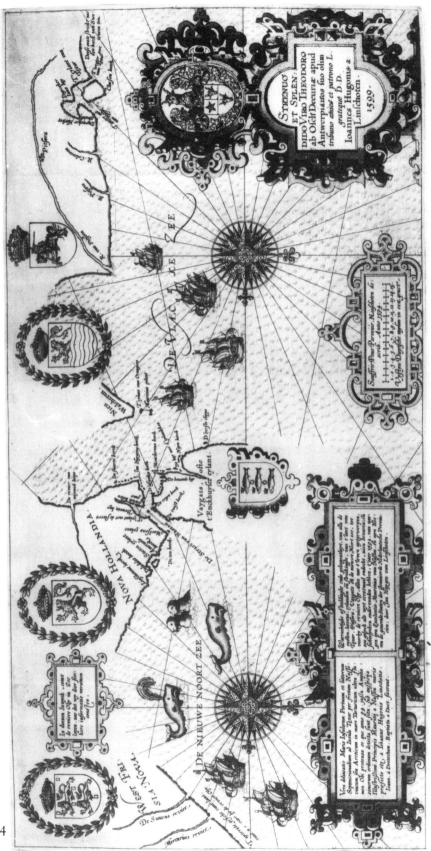

134

46.   (Illustration page 134.)
      Jan Huyghen van Linschoten, *The Voyage of 1594.*
      In Nassau Strait, between Vaygach and the north coast of Russia, a number of landfalls are
      indicated: Idol Point, Cross Point, Dispute Point, Barrel Point.

precious than that from elephants. They shot at the animal, then a group of six attacked it with harpoons and axes. But its powerful jaws bent the harpoons as if they were no more than sewing needles. It even began to push up against the side of the boat, biting and pulling at the rigging as if to make them capsize. After an hour and a half of struggle the men were happy to be rid of it again. They also found large quantitites of rock crystal, although of a very brittle variety, undoubtedly because of the cold climate. Here and there they also came across more religious statues. And occasionally they saw a beacon of stones piled up on the shore, evidence of some form of seafaring, even though they did not encounter a single boat. The waters were easily navigable, without reefs or sandbanks, and the small amounts of ice still floating in the area broke up and melted before their eyes.

They reached the Ob' estuary, a vast bay which proved to be rather shallow and to all appearances hardly navigable for ships of any size. This spelled the end of any hope for a route to Cathay by way of this river. Beyond the Ob' the coastline did indeed curve to the north. That was clearly where Tabin had to be. There was no more ice, the coast was low and flat, the sea wide and open. Linschoten, De la Dale, Tetgales and Nay together decided that they had done enough exploring. The northern passage had been discovered. If they were to sail any farther they would run the risk of finding the strait at Vaygach frozen over when they returned. It was time to go back.

But at Vaygach, too, there was no longer any sign of ice. All those huge icebergs, big as islands with their own hills and mountains, looking as if they were hundreds of years old, had simply disappeared, melted away to nothing in a matter of days. An amazing phenomenon, and reason to give thanks to the Creator. Continuing westward they met the ships of Barents which had gone as far as the seventy-eighth parallel, but had failed to find a passage because of excessive ice. So they returned as they had left, with all four ships dropping anchor at Texel on Friday, the sixteenth of September. [83]

All in all it had been a very satisfactory voyage. But some members of the Provincial Council of Holland still doubted whether it was really possible to follow the route around Tabin.[84] Some even said the expedition had returned too soon to be sure.[85] De Moucheron was furious. He believed that Plancius was behind the dissent again, and he may have been right. The Amsterdam clergyman had finally come out with his maps based on Mercator's system of increasing degrees; they would make it possible, he claimed, to determine longitude at sea according to the method of Lakeman.[86] He was convinced that they could now plot a much more certain course to Cathay than before.

---

83   Linschoten 1914, p. 37-114, 136.
84   Veer 2 1917, p. 236-239.
85   Stoppelaer 1901, p. 105; cf. Linschoten 1914, p. 137.
86   Keuning 1946, p. 89-91; Wieder 1 1925, p. 40.

And a much faster one, because ships could simply leave the safe coastline behind them and sail across open sea just south of the pole.

This time, however, De Moucheron was not about to let him go unchallenged. Through Valcke he approached Emanuel van Meteren, a close relative of Ortelius who had settled in London as a merchant and who spent his leisure time writing history. Van Meteren was told to get in touch with Richard Hakluyt, known to be still at work on his collection of travel accounts.[87] He, if anyone, would have at his finger tips all the literature needed to persuade the gentlemen, from reports of the ancient Greeks to the most recent travel accounts.

The plan brought results. Hakluyt was prepared to make available to them all his information about the northeast sea routes for the price of one hundred forty guilders. He traveled to London on horseback to discuss the matter and give them an overview. He not only had writings of the ancient Greeks and Romans at his disposal, but also accounts like the one by Johannes de Plano de Carpiny, who had ventured out to that part of the world more than three centuries earlier, even before Marco Polo. He did not, as was generally assumed, follow the southern route via Astrakhan and Bogar, but went farther north along what he called the Scythian Ocean. Hakluyt also appeared to have excerpts from the work of the fourteenth century Arab geographer Abulfeda, about which both Postel and Mercator had, in their time, expressed great curiosity.[88] And excerpts from the three volumes of Ramusius. This last work had been printed, but was very difficult to find.

Hakluyt himself, Van Meteren wrote, was convinced that Ortelius—and, for that matter most of the other geographers—had been seriously mistaken, and that ships could easily sail through to Cathay once they passed Vaygach. Beyond the Ob' the sea would be warmer and ice would no longer be a problem. The only danger was the Russians. Not the Tartars, whom he considered a much more trustworthy people.[89]

Once again De Moucheron put everything in writing. From Haithon the Armenian to Paulus Jovius, a long line of witnesses testified to the feasibility of sailing around Tabin. And it was confirmed by what the natives of those regions had told Brunel and, later, De la Dale. Besides, a Chinese ship had once been driven by a storm onto the German coast. It would be necessary, of course, to garrison troops on Vaygach in order to prevent the Russians, or anyone else, from blocking the passage. Traders could spend the winter there and transfer their cargoes, a proposal he had made earlier with regard to Kolguyev, and it should even be possible to establish a trading and fishing post there. For even if they never succeeded in sailing to China the fur trade and the whaling industry in the Tartar Ocean would be lucrative enough.[90]

- "So now what?"
- "Delay. The Zeelanders want to go but the Hollanders need time to think."
- "About what?"
- "Everything. Letting other private merchants take part, building fortifications—and about the route, of course."

---

87 Verduyn 1926, p. 150-151 and 163; Wallis 1984, p. 453.
88 Durme 1959, nr. 143, p. 159; Ortelius 1887, nr. 19, p. 42-43.
89 Veer 2 1917, p. 201-210.
90 Linschoten 1914, p. 231-242.

47. Gerrit de Veer, Levinus Hulsius, *The Voyage of 1595: The Collision*.
Four men drowned when Linschoten's and Barents' ships collided.

– "But time is pressing."
– "I know."

There were meetings with the Stadholder, with the Provincial Council of Holland, with the Provincial Council of Zeeland and with the States-General. Finally it was agreed that this time all the ships would take the route along Vaygach. From there to Kinsai was thought to be a matter of two weeks. Only on the return trip would the smaller ships, which in any case would not be carrying any goods, be allowed to explore the passage above Novaya Zemlya. The Amsterdammers even offered an extra premium of one thousand guilders for this venture.

– "They just won't take no for an answer."

But more delays followed. Inviting merchants to invest in the expedition, mustering the crew, writing the sailing instructions—all this took a disproportionate amount of time.[91] They finally set sail one month later than the year before. One month too late.[92] The voyage proved disastrous in every way. Soon after passing North Cape the ships of Linschoten and Barents collided simply because they each refused to allow the other to take the lead; four men drowned (see ill. 47). For one and half hours, with the ships locked together and a storm raging around them, despair reigned on board, and no one made any attempt to steer the vessels or adjust the sails. Finally the wind died

91   Stoppelaer 1901, p. 112-122; Veer 2 1917, p. 218-224.
92   Linschoten 1914, p. 138-141.

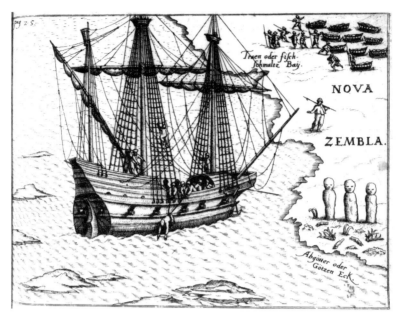

48.   Gerrit de Veer, Levinus Hulsius, *The Voyage of 1595: The Keelhauling*.
Two crewmen who stole pelts from the Lapps are keelhauled. One of them surfaces as
only half a body, the other is set ashore in his wet clothes.

down and the ships, almost miraculously, floated free. Once at Nassau Strait, two of the
crew members who were taking part in a land expedition stole some hides left behind
by the fleeing Lapps. As punishment they were keelhauled three times (see ill. 48). All
that surfaced of one of them was half a body. The other survived the ordeal but was set
ashore, wet as he was. The ships sailed on, braving storms and ice, but when they finally
reached the Tartar Sea, they managed to put only a few miles behind them before the
winds drove them back to the middle of Nassau Strait.

For seven days they were stranded between two dead whales in an inlet which they
christened Whale Oil Bay (see ill. 49). Many died from the stench of the rotting carcases, or from the heavy fog, also saturated with the stench, which formed drops as
large as a man's fist. De la Dale remembered Brunel's stories about the notorious "sea
lung" of mist and snow which he had encountered between seventy-five and seventy-
six degrees north latitude while on his mission to find Greenland for the Danish king—
he had seen people literally suffocate in the fog. Especially the landlubbers—craftsmen,
diamond cutters and goldsmiths, as well as envoys and passengers, the Amsterdam ship
in particular was full of them—died like flies. They would be walking, or talking, one
minute, and simply falling down dead the next. And no matter how well their bodies
were covered with stones, the bears dug them out at night and made a gruesome show,
dragging them around in a half-eaten state.

They did make a crossing to the mainland, and there François de la Dale, whose
long stay in Russia made him the most fluent speaker of Russian, talked at length with
the Lapps and was told once again about the coastline that curved to the north beyond

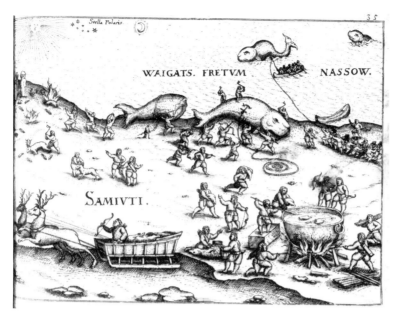

49. Gerrit de Veer, Levinus Hulsius, *The Voyage of 1595: The Whales*.
In Whale Oil Bay many on board died from the stench of rotting whale carcases.

the Ob', and about the open sea that stretched out from there.[93] They reached the Tartar Sea again as well. But by then it was already September. There was much too much ice to sail any farther, and the fog was so thick that they had to shoot cannons and muskets to identify their positions and prevent collisions. The arctic night was starting to fall. Drifting ice scraped against the ships…

Finally they reached Staten Island. The crew had no desire to go any farther, especially after two of them had been killed by a polar bear. There were stirrings of unrest. And while the captains, helmsmen, and merchants were meeting in the admiral's cabin to decide whether to stay where they were or return home, an uprising seemed imminent. It was quickly quelled and the five leaders were hanged on hastily erected gallows hammered together from floating wreckage (see ill. 50). But then they did set out for home after all. Barents came along, even though he had first proposed to stay behind with two ships and spend the winter there. No one could understand what he hoped to achieve by doing so, and he might not have been clear about it himself, for when finally, after several failed attempts, they managed to make their way back through Nassau Strait, he no longer talked about a more northern route and set sail for Holland no less cheerfully than the others, as if there were no reward to be claimed for further explorations.[94]

They returned home on October 26, 1595 with nothing more to show for their voyage than the two gigantic jawbones which Jan Huyghen van Linschoten had ordered removed from a dead whale. They were placed on display in the shooting gallery and city hall of Enkhuizen in lasting memory of the expedition.[95]

93   Linschoten 1914, p. 169-172 and 276-277.
94   Burger 1920a, p. 211-223. Cf. also Linschoten 1914, p. 149-185 and Veer 1 1917, p. 28-45.
95   Linschoten 1914, p. 180-188 and 271-272.

50. Gerrit de Veer, Levinus Hulsius, *The Voyage of 1595: The Rebellion.*
    Unrest breaks out after two men out hunting for rock crystal are killed by a polar bear.
    Five rabble-rousers are hanged.

> – "But the Lapps said it had been an extremely harsh winter and the summer was colder than anyone could remember. Next time things will certainly be easier."
> – "No, François."
> – "Jan Huyghen thinks so. He says the Portuguese didn't make all their discoveries on their first try either, but year after year they sent out new expeditions, in spite of the high cost—so it would be a shame to give up now, after all the efforts and investments that have been made so far."[96]
> – "No."

A combination of factors steered the decision. While the second voyage was still under way, Melchior de Moucheron had managed to secure an extremely promising trade agreement with the Russians. He was unwilling to place that in the balance for an expedition which the tsar, fearful of a Dutch monopoly in Nassau Strait, eyed with great suspicion, and which in any case offered no sure results. At the same time the chances of finding a sea route around Africa seemed to be growing. In April of 1595 De Houtman had set out with four ships to explore the possibilities in that direction. If they were to prove favorable it would be important to start exploiting them as soon as possible, and for that they would need money, a great deal of money. No, this was really not the moment to go off on more arctic adventures. François had to return to Moscow to assist Melchior, so that he could eventually take over his post there.[97]

---

96   Linschoten 1914, p. 206-208 and 281.
97   Bartelds 1927, col. 889; Linschoten 1914, p. lxxii.

The Provincial Councils of Zeeland and Holland were not prepared to finance a third voyage either. The only thing which the States-General decided to grant, on the suggestion of Holland, was a premium of twenty-five thousand guilders plus two years exemption from import and export tariffs for anyone who opened up the passage at their own expense. For the municipal government of Amsterdam this was reason enough to equip two ships of their own for one more attempt—"in view of the great importance for the commonweal," as they put it.[98]

This time Plancius' ideas would be given free rein. The learned doctor Paludanus from Enkhuizen, a friend of Linschoten, wrote to Ortelius in Antwerp that Plancius and Barents were convinced that a passage could be found in the north, because God, as everyone knew, had surrounded the earth with water, and the current in that region alternated, flowing first to the east, then to the west. Also significant was that the north winds there were warmer than those from the south. If there was such a place as the peninsula Tabin, they maintained, it had to be Novaya Zemlya.[99]

51. Gerrit de Veer, *The Voyage of 1596: The Sign in the Sky*.
Early in the voyage a strange sign appears in the sky, with three suns and four rainbows. It is believed to be a good omen.

---

98   Linschoten 1914, p. lxx; Veer 2 1917, p. 235-236.
99   Ortelius 1887, nr. 285, p. 678; Tracy 1980, p. 38-39 and 56.

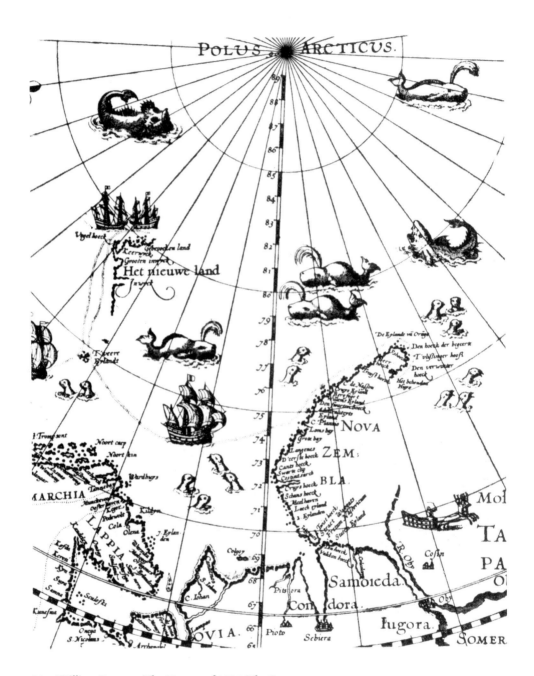

52. William Barents, *The Voyage of 1596: The Route*.
Once past Norway, Barents, Heemskerck and De Rijp continue north instead of follow-ing the coastline. They reach Bear Island and Spitsbergen (The New Land) but then have to turn back. At Bear Island they split up: De Rijp goes west, Barents and Heemskerck east, toward Novaya Zemlya.

The idea of a whirlpool which sucked all the gulf streams of the world inside the earth had died out long ago—no one had taken it seriously since the books of Peter Martyr.[100] But now the four polar islands, which had been a standard element of arctic geography since Mercator, were brushed aside as well, and no one so much as mentioned a magnetic mountain at the pole or in the Strait of Anian anymore.[101]

On May 18, 1596 they once again set sail for the north, in two ships with Jacob Heemskerck and Jan Corneliszoon de Rijp serving as captains, and with Willem Barents in charge of the entire expedition.[102]

The mysterious configuration of three suns and four rainbows which appeared in the sky on June 4, when they had reached the seventy-first parallel, had to be a favorable omen (see ill. 51). But by the next day they had already encountered their first icebergs. The following days brought them through more ice, which meant that they could not be far from land. This led Barents to suspect that they had sailed too far to the west and that they were now in the vicinity of Greenland. De Rijp believed none of this, but on June 10th they did indeed come upon land (see ill. 52).

It was an island. They named it Bear Island, after their encounter with a polar bear: although the ten men in the rowboat were armed with guns and axes, they struggled for two full hours before the bear was dead. Six days later they reached another coast, which stretched on up to the eightieth parallel, and possibly even farther.[103] De Rijp christened it The New Land, and the sailors referred to it as Spitsbergen, because of the mountains there that reached the clouds.

- – "Mount Stolp?"
- – "Who knows."

But now Barents was sure—this had to be Greenland.[104] The same Greenland as in the Bardsen descriptions which he owned. But they were now at a much more northern point, somewhere near the island of Margaster and the St. Thomas monastery, where the monks raised their vegetables in the warmth of the volcano.

They could, of course, have viewed this as a success, finding the land which for more than a century had eluded not only Pining and Pothorst, but also the archbishop of Trondheim, Erik Walkendorf, and later Olivier Brunel as well. Perhaps King Christian IV of Denmark would follow the example of his predecessors and offer a handsome reward. But the assignment had been to find a route to China.

So they returned to Bear Island. From there Barents wanted to chart a course more to the northeast. De Rijp, however, kept insisting that they would have to pass The New Land on the west side if they wanted to get near the pole. Angry words were exchanged. From high up in the officers' quarters their voices carried over the water. In the end the only solution was for each to go his own way.[105]

---

100 See chapter II, p. 39.
101 Burger 1915, p. 322-325; Burger 1920b, p. 272.
102 Veer 2 1917, p. xxxix; Burger 1920b, p. 333.
103 Veer 1 1917, p. 46-54; Veer 2 1917, p. lxiii-lxiv.
104 Veer 2 1917, p. 244-245; Burger 1920b, p. 338-339.
105 Veer 1 1917, p. 55.

53.   Gerrit de Veer. *The Voyage of 1596: The Ship on the Ice.*
Past the northern tip of Novaya Zemlya ice floes close in and the ship is forced up onto the ice.

Jan Corneliszoon de Rijp sailed his ship one hundred fifty miles through icebergs. Floes knocked a hole in the hull, making it necessary for them to pump continuously as they went on. Finally they reached open water. There they moved all the goods, anchors, cables and guns to one side of the ship, causing it to list; this allowed them to repair the hole from the outside using the ship's boat. They then sailed on until, at the eighty-first parallel, they once again touched land. This time De Rijp was also convinced that he had reached Greenland.

It was warm there, just as the old stories described it. So warm that at night, with the sun still high in the sky, that the men slept on deck. Wildlife abounded: walruses with their precious tusks, polar bears, birds, and on the land reindeer and foxes and martens. They even saw hoofprints of horses. Some of the men thought they had to be unicorns, although these were always pictured with cloven hooves. And what had Pliny written—something about islands in the far north where the natives had horses' hooves instead of feet?[106]

But there was no way to sail around it. Twelve weeks they spent searching for a passage as far as the eighty-fourth parallel, but all they found was land. And ice. Not a human being to be seen, to say nothing of settlements or monasteries, or even a few Skraeling huts. Finally, like all the others before them, they had to turn back, their mission unaccomplished.[107]

---

106   See chapter V, p. 96.
107   Veer 2 1917, p. lxiv-lxvii; Ortelius 1887, nr. 298, p. 89; cf. Tracy 1980, p. 58.

54. Gerrit de Veer, Levinus Hulsius, *The Voyage of 1596: The Cabin Called "Safe House"*.
They used wood from the ship and wreckage from the shore to build a shelter.

Barents and Heemskerck's ship passed the northern point of Novaya Zemlya, which they believed to be Cape Tabin, then became icebound (see ill. 53). They must have seen it coming. For three weeks the ice had been drifting up against the ship, but Barents had not said a word about turning back. His proposal of the previous year—to spend the winter on Staten Island so that they would be able to sail on at the first opportunity in the spring—had been rejected, but now he saw his chance. This might even explain why he steered toward land instead of staying out in the open sea where he knew there would be less ice. Finally, as if lifted by some giant lever, the ship moved up onto the ice, leaving them no alternative: they would spend the winter there.

From August 30, 1596 to June 14 of the following year Novaya Zemlya was their home. They built a cabin using wood from the ship and from wreckage which they found washed ashore (see ill. 54). Each day they carved a notch into one of the beams, now and then they shot a bear or caught a fox in one of their traps; for the rest they were cooped up inside, telling stories and waiting for the sun to return. On one occasion, when they burned coal from the ship's stores instead of collecting driftwood for their fire, they nearly died of carbon monoxide poisoning. Otherwise very little happened.

Finally the sun came back and the bears reappeared, chasing the foxes into their holes. But as the weather grew steadily warmer the ship did not float free. At the end of March the movement of the water actually pushed it farther up on the ice, and despite all that Barents had hoped to achieve, they had no choice but to attempt a return to the civilized world with the crew and all the goods in two open boats (see ill. 55).

It was a terrible journey, cold and wet, and even in midsummer repeatedly threatened by ice. For one and a half months they followed the coast, from the Island of

145

55.   Gerrit de Veer, *The Voyage of 1596: The Return.*
      The following spring they begin their return trip in two open boats. Barents dies along the
      way.

Orange to Ice Point, from Ice Point to Bear Point, from Bear Point to Cape Comfort, then on along the places familiar to Barents from two years before, as far as Costins Serch, known from Olivier Brunel's travels, and on again from there (see ill. 56).[108]

They finally reached Kildin on August 25.[109] Barents himself did not survive the trip. But up to the very moment of his death he kept insisting that there was a route past the pole through open sea, and that he would find it the next time. Was it not true that ventures often failed on the first, second, or even third attempt, but in the end were crowned with success? Great discoveries seldom resulted from a single effort. No blame should be attached to those who undertook the seemingly impossible, only to those who through indolence or lack of courage never made such attempts.[110]

   –   "And Gog and Magog? And the ten tribes of Israel? And Mount Stolp with
       Hyperboreans living at its foot? And Paradise?"[111]
   –   "Nonsense. Book learning. Only experience and mathematics, the accurate
       measuring of latitude and longitude, can tell us what the world is really like."[112]
   –   "Calculating longitude at sea—that secret still hasn't been discovered, even
       though Plancius and Lakeman claim otherwise. Poor De Rijp, his longitudinal

---

108   Veer 1 1917, p. 18-22.
109   Veer 1 1917, p. 60-170.
110   Veer 1 1917, p. 1-4.
111   See chapter IV, p. 80-82 and VI, p. 126-127.
112   Linschoten 1914, p. 27; Veer 1 1917, p. xx and p. 2-3.

indicator led him way off course. When he thought he was entering the White Sea he ended up on the Lofotens, and the course he had charted under the pole brought him into the ice near Greenland."[113]

 – "De Rijp had no idea how to use their method. He should have listened to Barents instead of feeling so sure of himself."
 – "As if anyone knows where Greenland is. And is if there's anything but ice in that whole part of the world. Sebastian Cabot found that out, and since then no one has discovered anything different. Just ice, ice, and more ice."

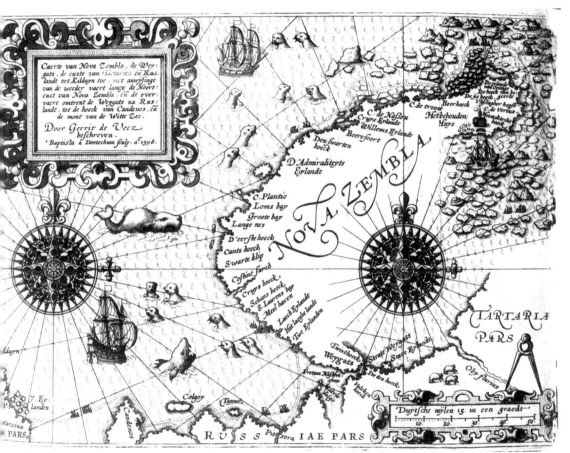

56.   Gerrit de Veer, *The Voyage of 1596: The Return Route.*
     For one and a half months they follow the coastline: from Safe House past the Island of Orange, Ice Point, Bear Point, and Cape Comfort to Costins Serch. From there they sail past Kolguyev directly to Kola.

---

113   Veer 2 1917, p. xxi-xxviii and lxi; Keuning 1946, p. 123-127.

Epilogue

In 1597 a book of twenty pages written by Mathijs Syvertszoon Lakeman was published in Amsterdam. Besides describing the travels of a certain Mathias Sofridus, it explained in detail the method which he had developed for determining longitude at sea (see ill. 57).

This Sofridus, the story went, had commissioned a ship to be built for the purpose of sailing around the world. The vessel was constructed completely of whalebone, both inside and out. It had the form of an English warship, with its low bow and high stern, its

57. *The Treatise of Mathijs Syvertszoon Lakeman.*
   Title page of the book which recounts the amazing voyage of Mathias Sofridus.

striking colors, and six heavy guns. But he also ordered the construction of four large blades resembling those of a windmill, complete with sails, as well as two large wheels and one small one studded with spikes. All this he stowed on the deck of his ship.

Equipped in this way he set sail from Enkhuizen on December 12, 1595, with a helmsman named Pamanus. On the 24th of December they passed North Cape and set course for Nassau Strait. They had gone only half way when they encountered ice—four fathoms thick it was, and solidly packed as far as the eye could see. Sofridus dropped anchor. He attached the windmill blades to the main mast, the large wheels to the two sides of the hull, and the small wheel back near the rudder. He then allowed the ship to move up onto the ice, a relatively easy maneuver with those spiked wheels. They weighed anchor. And unfurled the sails. The wind caught them, and there they went, as fast as if two horses were pulling them, and as smoothly as a cart on a sandy road.

The crew had the time of their lives, and stayed on deck even though there was no more work for them to do. The captain shouted:

- "Maybe we'll find St. Patrick's purgatory—they say it's somewhere just south of the pole."

And one of the men replied:

- "Yes, we will. Once when I was sailing along the coast of Norway with a stiff north wind we met a ship with a south wind in its sails. We shouted: 'What is your cargo?' And the men on that ship shouted back: 'The toll collector of the Sont.' And when we arrived there four days later we found out that the collector of the royal Sont toll had died around that time."

With tall tales like this one they passed their time. After Nassau Strait, where they saw a frozen polar bear standing upright on the ice, they went on past Staten Island, past the Ob' and finally reached the promontory of Tabin (see ill. 58).

There they came upon a narrow strait. At first they thought it was a river, but on realizing that its ice was salty, they knew that there had to be another sea at the opposite end. The passage was broader than Nassau Strait and about ten miles long. It did indeed lead to a sea, one so huge that no land was visible anywhere, neither on the port nor on the starboard side.

They sailed due east. After a few days they caught sight of a mountain gleaming in the sun, as high as one of the three Drommels in Norway. As they came nearer, they saw that it was solid lodestone. Unswervingly the ship with all its bolts and nails and iron was drawn towards it. On checking their position they found that they were at seventy-three degrees north latitude. Sofridus maintained that there had to be an identical mountain at the same latitude in the southern hemisphere, because in both the north and the south compass needles pointed in that direction.

How they managed to break free the story does not tell. In any case they eventually sailed on, still in an easterly direction, and still on ice—until they reached the meridian of California. They then steered a course to the south. For several days they skimmed over vast frozen seas, then followed a coastline and entered another strait, which led them to a wide sea surrounded by mountains. There they finally dismantled their windmill and raised the sails.

58. Gerard Mercator, *Asia* (1595).
The route followed by Mathias Sofridus can be traced here: along the southern coast of
Vaygach, past the Ob' estuary, the Isthmus of Tabin and the Magnetic Mountain, into the
Strait of Anian.

150

58a. Detail from illustration 58.

It was two days later that they were caught off guard by a tremendous roar, like that of an approaching storm. The noise came toward them so quickly that panic broke out on board. Then they saw it—the god Neptune was chasing a walrus. The helmsman Pamanus took aim with his musket from the forecastle and shot the animal through the head. Neptune was extremely grateful, for his dogs and horses were exhausted, and the walrus, which had caused a great deal of damage in his fishing waters, would otherwise surely have escaped. He invited them to follow him, and after sailing a day and a half they arrived at his castle. It stood tall on a coral rock in the middle of the sea. All the buildings, walls and towers were made of different colors of coral and were decorated in the tradition of the ancients with pearl and mother of pearl and an endless variety of seashells.

They disembarked and were welcomed by Fantano, Neptune's helmsman, who gave them a tour of the castle and then invited them to join Neptune for a meal. After some time at the table, Neptune began to ask questions: how had they managed to enter his sea where no human being had ever been before; and what kind of instruments and skills did they have at their disposal. Mathias Sofridus answered as best he could. He also told of how people had tried to find the philosophers' stone, which was believed to possess power to transform ordinary metal into gold and to heal all diseases. Many had sacrificed their money, property, and health in this pursuit. Neptune laughed and asked if they did not know what had happened to their ancestors when they tried to build the Tower of Babel. Hours passed as they talked. Eventually mermaids brought out their instruments and struck up music more beautiful than any of the men had ever heard.

When Fantano later led them to the room where they would sleep, Mathias Sofridus took him aside and asked if he, as Neptune's helmsman, knew how to determine longitude at sea, adding that he had undertaken this journey out of a desire to learn how it might be done. Fantano laughed:

– "Then you've come to the right man, because I deal with this every day. Tomorrow I'll explain it to you in all its details, but first let's first get some sleep."

And indeed, the next day Fantano took them into a room full of instruments and maps of all kinds; there they sat down and he explained everything just as he had promised.

The explanation given by Fantano was recounted at some length by Mathijs Lakeman, complete with examples and anecdotes. Fantano told of how he had once reached Iceland in half the time he had originally calculated, and how a similar miscalculation had landed him on the rocks near Norway, a mishap he had survived only by clinging to a floating plank. Such things would no longer happen now that there was a new method of calculation. He also described new types of navigation charts and the instruments which they required, such as a special kind of compass and quadrant, as well as three-armed compasses. And once it was all explained the author quoted Mathias Sofridus as saying that it was now time to take leave of their hosts and put this all to the test.

They set a course to the north, the direction from which they had come. Again they passed the magnetic pole—do not ask how—and the promontory of Tabin. Sailing along the Ob' estuary they witnessed a battle between the Tartars and the native Samoyeds, and saw how the latter used their magic to overturn the Tartar ships and set them ablaze. But the wind was favorable, so they left the skirmish behind them, speeding on across the ice, through Nassau Strait and into the Northern Sea, which was now known as Barents Sea. There they reached open water. Once again they dismantled the windmill construction, hauled the wheels up onto the deck and raised the sails. They returned to Enkhuizen, finally possessing the knowledge for which so many had searched for so long in vain.[1]

One year later Petrus Plancius and Mathijs Syvertszoon Lakeman officially requested the Provincial Council of Holland to reward them for their new method of determining longitude. A committee of scholars and cartographers was appointed and a broad discussion ensued about the merits of their discovery. A reward was never given.[2] But Plancius knew for sure that this was the dawn of a new age, a new millenium perhaps, in which all prophecies would be fulfilled, and that his vision of ships sailing over the North Pole would become a reality.

---

1   Lakeman 1597, passim; cf. Burger 1930, p. 133-148.
2   Wieder 1 1925, p. 40; Keuning 1946, p. 131-133.

Acknowledgements

With thanks to Jan Werner and Kees Scheide of the map collection and Iman Heijstek of the photography department of the University of Amsterdam library, also to Barbara Heezen for her photocopies of the English *State Papers*, Leo Noordegraaf for information about the Asian caravan routes, Willem Weststeijn for the translation of a Russian text, Chris Heesakkers for the translation of a Latin text, Frieda van Noordwijk for information about the battle at Fotvig, Anja Muller and Caroline Gautier for assistance with the illustrations, Annelies van Hees, Mieke Smits-Veldt, and Annette Portegies, for a number of stylistic corrections, and Natascha Veldhorst for stylistic suggestions and especially for her help with the expansion and correction of the notes.

Literature

Adam von Bremen 1917
    Adam von Bremen, *Hamburgische Kirchengeschichte*. Ed. Bernhard Schmeidler. Hannover
    and Leipzig 1917.
Ahvenainen 1967
    Jorma Ahvenainen, *Some contributions to the question of Dutch traders in Lapland and Rus-
    sia at the end of the sixteenth century*. Rovaniemi 1967 (Acta Lapponica Fenniae 6).
Armstrong 1984
    T. Armstrong, 'In search of a sea route to Siberia, 1553-1619.' In: *Arctic* 37, 4 (1984), p. 429-
    440.
Bächtold-Stäubli 1931-32
    H. Bächtold-Stäubli, a.o. (eds.), *Handwörterbuch des deutschen Aberglaubens*. Vol. 4. Berlin
    and Leipzig 1931-32.
Bagrow 1962
    Leo Bagrow, 'At the sources of the cartography of Russia.' In: *Imago mundi* 16 (1962),
    p. 33-48.
Bagrow 1964
    Leo Bagrow, *History of cartography*. Revised and enlarged by R.A. Skelton. London 1964.
Bartelds 1927
    J.C.E. Bartelds, 'Melchior de Moucheron.' In: P.C. Molhuysen a.o. (eds.), *Nieuw Neder-
    lands biografisch woordenboek*. Vol. 7 Leiden 1927, kol. 888-890.
Becanus 1569
    Joan. Goropius Becanus, *Origines Antwerpianae, sive Cimmeriorum becceselana novem
    libros complexa*. Antverpiae 1569.
Berens 1968
    Willy Berens, 'Ein grosser Eupener: Gillis Hooftman.' In: *Geschichtliches Eupen* 2 (1968),
    p. 56-81.
Borst 1 1957, 2.1 1958, 2.2. 1959, 3.1 1960
    Arno Borst, *Der Turmbau von Babel. Geschichte der Meinungen über Ursprung und
    Vielfalt der Sprachen und Völker*. 4 vols. Stuttgart 1957-63.
Bostoen 1984
    K. Bostoen, *Kaars en bril: de oudste Nederlandse grammatica*. Archief van het Koninklijk
    Zeeuws Genootschap der Wetenschappen 1984.
Boumans 1954
    René Boumans, 'The religious views of Abraham Ortelius.' In: *Warburg journal* 17 (1954),
    p. 374-377.
Bourne 1599
    W. Bourne, *De const der zee-vaerdt* [etc.]. *midsgaders een bequaem Hydrographical dis-
    course, om door 5. verscheyden wegen na Cathaia ende China te seylen*. Amsterdam 1599.

Bouwsma 1957
W.J. Bouwsma, *Concordia mundi. The career and thought of Guillaume Postel (1501-1581)*. Cambridge, Mass. 1957.

Brandaan 1978
De reis van Sinte Brandaan. Ed. Maartje Draak. Herdicht door Bertus Aafjes. 2nd ed. Amsterdam 1978.

Brandmair 1914
Eduard Brandmair, *Bibliographische Untersuchungen über Entstehung und Entwicklung des Ortelischen Kartenwerkes*. München 1914.

Brouwer 1953
P.C. de Brouwer, 'Joannes Goropius Becanus, een der Brabantse humanisten uit de zestiende eeuw.' In: *Brabantia* 2 (1953), p. 270-281.

Brulez 1959
W. Brulez, *De firma Della Faille en de internationale handel van Vlaamse firma's in de 16e eeuw*. Brussel 1959 (Verh. Kon. Vl. Ac. v. Wet. Let. en Sch. K. 35).

Burger 1915
C.P. Burger jr., 'De Noordpoolstreken op onze 16e-eeuwse kaarten.' In: *Het boek* NR 4 (1915), p. 209-216, 260-267 318-325 en 377-384.

Burger 1916
C.P. Burger jr., 'De oudste Hollandsche wereldkaart. Een werk van Cornelius Aurelius.' In: *Het boek* NR 5 (1916), p. 34-66.

Burger 1920a
C.P. Burger jr., 'De poolzee-reis van 1595.' In: *Het boek* NR 9 (1920), p. 209-228 en 242-251.

Burger 1920b
C.P. Burger jr., 'De poolzee-reis van 1596.' In: *Het boek* NR 9 (1920), p. 273-288 en 331-355.

Burger 1928
C.P. Burger jr., 'Een werk van Willem Barents teruggevonden.' In: *Het boek* 17 (1928), p. 225-240.

Burger 1930
C.P. Burger jr., *De deurvaert by noorden om naar Cathay ende China*. 's-Gravenhage 1930. (Offprints from *Het boek* 1929-30).

Cabot 1544 (1968)
Sébastien Cabot, *Mappemonde*. Paris 1968.

Cipolla 1973
Carlo M. Cipolla (ed.), *The Fontana economic history of Europe. The Middle Ages*. 2nd ed. London 1973.

Coornaert 1 1961, 2 1961
Emile Coornaert, *Les Français et le commerce international à Anvers, fin du XVe-XVIe siècle*. 2 vols. Paris 1961.

Coote 1886
C.H. Coote, 'Sebastian Cabot, 1474-1557' In: *Dictionary of national biography*. Vol. 8. London 1886, p. 166-171.

Cordt 1891
B. Cordt, 'Beiträge zu einer Russisch-Niederländischen Bibliographie.' In: C.C. Uhlenbeck, *Verslag aangaande een onderzoek in de archieven van Rusland ten bate der Nederlandse geschiedenis*. 's-Gravenhage 1891.

Couvreur 1975
[W. Couvreur (ed.)] *Antwerpen in de 16e eeuw*. Antwerpen 1975.

Decleringe 1 1983, 2 1983
Een corte decleringhe deser spere. Ed. Utrechtse neerlandici. 2 vols. Utrecht 1983.

Denucé 1 1912, 2 1913
　　Jan Denucé, *Oud-Nederlandsche kaartmakers in betrekking met Plantijn*. 2 vols. Antwerpen, 's-Gravenhage 1912, 1913.
Denucé (1938)
　　J. Denucé, *Afrika in de XVIde eeuw en de handel van Antwerpen*. 's-Gravenhage (1938).
Destombes 1970
　　M. Destombes, 'An Antwerp unicum: an unpublished terrestial globe of the 16th century in the Bibliotheque Nationale, Paris.' In: *Imago mundi* 24 (1970), p. 85-94.
Destombes 1985
　　M. Destombes, 'Guillaume Postel cartographe.' In: *Guillaume Postel 1581-1981. Actes du colloque international d'Avranches 1981*. Paris 1985, p. 361-371.
Dorsten 1973
　　J.A. van Dorsten, *The radical arts. First decade of an Elisabethan renaissance*. 2nd ed. Leiden, London 1973.
Dreyer-Eimbcke 1994
　　Oswald Dreyer-Eimbcke, 'Durchs Eis ins Reich der Mitte, Einfluß und Bedeutung der Kartographie bei der Such nach den Nordpassagen, von der Anfängen bis zum Ende des 16. Jahrhunderts.' In: Ruth Löffler, Gernot Tromnau a.o.
　　(eds.), *Gerhard Mercator, Europa und die Welt. Ausstellung Duisburg 1994-1995*. Duisburg 1994, p. 131-171.
Dubois 1972
　　C-G. Dubois, *Celtes et Gaulois au XVIe siècle. Le développement littéraire d'un mythe nationaliste. Avec l'édition critique d'un traité inédit de Guillaume Postel 'De ce qui est premier pour reformer le monde'*. Paris 1972.
Durme 1959
　　M. van Durme (ed.), *Correspondance Mercatorienne*. Anvers 1959.
Fischer 1 1768
　　Johann Eberhard Fischer, *Sibirische Geschichte von der Entdekkung Sibiriens bis auf die Eroberung dieses Lands durch die Russische Waffen* [etc.]. Vol. 1. Sint Petersburg 1768.
Fisher 1943
　　Raymond H. Fisher, *The Russian fur trade 1550-1700*. Berkeley and Los Angeles 1943 (Univ. of California publications in history 31).
Franck 1595
　　Sebastiaen Franck, *Werelt-boeck. Spieghel ende Beeltenisse des geheelen Aerdtbodems* [etc.]. Amsterdam 1595.
French 1984
　　Peter J. French, *John Dee. The world of an Elizabethan magus*. 2nd ed. London 1984.
Geiger 1886
　　Ludwig Geiger, 'Sebastian Münster.' In: *Allgemeine Deutsche Biographie*. Vol. 23. Leipzig 1886, p. 30-33.
Geske 1962
　　H.H. Geske, 'Die Vita Mercatoris des Walter Ghim.' In: *Duisburger Forschungen* 6 (1962), p. 244-276.
Grobecker 1979
　　Manfred Grobecker, 'Albert Krantz.' In: *Neue Deutsche Biographie*. Vol. 12. Berlin 1979, p. 673-674.
Groenveld-Leeuwenberg 1979
　　S. Groenveld, H.L.Ph. Leeuwenberg, a.o., *De kogel door de kerk? De opstand in de Nederlanden en de rol van de Unie van Utrecht, 1559-1609*. Zutphen 1979.
Gro(o)te, Olaus de
　　see: Magnus

Grynaeus 1532
   Simon Grynaeus, *Novus orbis regionum et insularum veteribus incognitarum* [etc.]. Parisiis 1532.
Guicciardini 1612
   L. Guicciardini, *Beschryvinghe van alle de Neder-Landen;* [etc.] Overgheset in de Neder-duytsche spraeck, door Corn. Kilianum. Vermeerdert ender verciert door P. Montanum. Amsterdam 1612.
Günther-Lauchert 1900
   Günther en Lauchert, 'Jakob Ziegler.' In: *Allgemeine Deutsche Biographie.* Vol. 45. Leipzig 1900, p. 176-177.
Hacquebord 1983
   Louwrens Hacquebord, 'Holland op z'n koudst. Het verloop van de zeventiende-eeuwse Nederlandse walvisvaart in de noordelijke ijszeeën.' In: Els Naayer (ed.), *Smeerenburg: Holland op z'n koudst.* Groningen 1983 (Mededelingen Arctisch centrum 7), p. 41-58.
Haecht 1 1929, 2 1933
   De kroniek van Godevaert van Haecht over de troebelen van 1565 tot 1574 te Antwerpen en elders. Ed. Rob. van Roosbroeck. 2 vols. Antwerpen 1929-33.
Haithonus-Grynaeus 1532
   Haithonus Armenus, *De Tartaris liber.* In: Simon Grynaeus, *Novus orbis regionum et insularum veteribus incognitarum* [etc.]. Parisiis 1532.
Hakluyt 1 1598
   Richard Hakluyt, *The principal navigations, voiages, traffiques and discoueries of the English nation* [etc.]. Vol. 1: 'Containing the woorthy discoueries etc. of the English toward the North and Northeast by sea [etc.].' 2nd ed. London 1598.
Hamann 1982
   Günther Hamann, 'Das Weltbild im 11. Jahrhundert im Rahmen der Kartographie des Mittelalters.' In: *Jahrbuch für Geschichte des Feudalismus* 6 (1982), p. 53-86.
Hamilton 1981
   Alastair Hamilton, *The family of love.* Cambridge 1981.
Heezen-Stoll 1990
   Barbara Heezen-Stoll, 'Johan Radermacher.' In: *Nationaal biografsch woordenboek.* Vol. 13. Brussel 1990, p. 673-680.
Hennig 1 1944, 2 1950, 3 1953, 4 1956
   R. Hennig, *Terrae incognitae. Eine Zusammenstellung und kritische Bewertung der wichtigsten vorcolumbischen Entdeckungsreisen an Hand der darüber vorliegenden Originalberichte.* 2nd rev. ed. 4 vols. Leiden 1944-56.
Henning 1906
   Georg Henning, *Reiseberichte über Siberien von Herberstein bis Ides.* Leipzig 1906.
Herberstein 1557
   Sigmundus Liberus [von Herberstein], *Rerum Moscoviticarum commentarri.* [etc.] Antverpiae 1557.
Héthoum
   see: Haithonus
Hintzsche 1994
   Wieland Hintzsche, 'Die kartographische Darstellung Sibiriens bei Gerhard Mercator.' In: Irmgard Hantsche (ed.), *Mercator - ein Wegbereiter neuzeitlichen Denkens.* Referate des 2. Mercator-Symposiums, Duisburg, 8-9 März 1993. Bochum 1994, p. 171-182.
Horensma 1985
   P.T.G. Horensma, 'Olivier Brunel and the Dutch involvement in the discovery of the Northeast passage.' In: *FRAM: the journal of polar studies* 2 (1985), p. 123-128.

Houtte 1963

J.A. van Houtte, *Gerard Mercator 1512-1594*. Herdenkingsrede uitgesproken ter gelegenheid van de 450ste verjaring van Mercators geboorte. Brussel 1963 (Kon. Vl. Ac. v. Wet., Let. en Sch. K.).

Jacob 1981

H.K. 's Jacob, 'Two images of the North Atlantic. Adam of Bremen (11th century) and Nicolò Zeno (16th century).' In: *Early European exploitation of the Northern Atlantic 800-1700. Proceedings of the international symposium. Arctic centre, februari 1981*. Groningen 1981, p. 7-25.

Jansma 1946

T.S. Jansma, 'Olivier Brunel te Dordrecht: de noordoostelijke doorvaart en het Westeuropeesch-Russisch contact in de zestiende eeuw.' In: *Tijdschrift voor geschiedenis* 59 (1946), p. 337-362.

Janssens-Uyttersprot 1990

J. Janssens, V. Uyttersprot, e.a., *En toch was ze rond... Middeleeuws mens- en wereldbeeld*. Brussel z.j. (1990).

Jauß 1970

Hans Robert Jauß, *Literaturgeschichte als Provokation*. Frankfurt am Main 1970.

Johannesson 1991

Kurt Johannesson, *The renaissance of the Goths in sixteenth-century Sweden. Johannes and Olaus Magnus as politicians and historians*. Transl. James Larson. Berkeley, Los Angeles, Oxford 1991.

Jovius-Grynaeus 1532

Paulus Jovius, *De legatione Moschovitarum libellus*. In: Simon Grynaeus, *Novus orbis regionum et insularum veteribus incognitarum* [etc.]. Parisiis 1532.

Karrow 1993

Robert W. Karrow., *Bio-bibliographies of the cartographers of Abraham Ortelius, 1570*. Based on Leo Bagrow's *A. Ortelii catalogus cartographorum*. Chicago 1993.

Kempers 1996

Bram Kempers, 'Een pauselijke opdracht. Het proto-museum van Julius II op de derde verdieping van het Vaticaans paleis.' In: Harald Hendrix and Jeroen Stumpel (eds.), *Kunstenaars en opdrachtgevers*. Amsterdam 1996, p. 7-48.

Kernkamp 1903

G.W. Kernkamp, *Verslag van een onderzoek in Zweden, Noorwegen en Denemarken naar archivalia, belangrijk voor de geschiedenis van Nederland*. 's-Gravenhage 1903.

Keuning 1946

J. Keuning, *Petrus Plancius, theoloog en geograaf, 1552-1622*. Amsterdam 1946.

Knauer 1981

Elfriede Regina Knauer, *Die Carte Marina des Olaus Magnus von 1539. Ein kartographisches Meisterwerk und seine Wirkung*. Göttingen 1981.

Krantzius 1583

Albertus Krantzius, *Regnorum aquilonarium, Daniae, Sueciae, Noruagiae, chronica* [etc]. Item *Iacobi Ziegleri Schondia, id est regionum et populorum septentrionalium, ad Krantzianam historiam perutilis descriptio*. Francofurti ad Moenum 1583.

Kretschmer 1995

Ingrid Kretschmer, 'Kartenprojektionen in Gerhard Mercators Atlas.' In: Hans H. Blotevogel and Rienk Vermij (eds.), *Gerhard Mercator und die geistige Strömungen des 16. und 17. Jahrhunderts*. Bochum 1995, p. 65-85.

Krogt 1994
> Peter van der Krogt, 'Erdgloben, Wandkarten, Atlanten. Gerhard Mercator kartiert die Erde.' In: Ruth Löffler, Gernot Tromnau a.o. (eds.), *Gerhard Mercator, Europa und die Welt. Ausstellung Duisburg 1994-1995*. Duisburg 1994, p. 81-129.

Kunz 1981
> Marion L. Kunz, *Guilllaume Postel, prophet of the Restitution of All Things. His life and thought*. The Hague, etc. 1981.

Lakeman 1597
> [Mathijs Syvertsz. Lakeman] *Een tractaet, seer dienstelijck voor alle zee-varende luyden* [etc.]. Amsterdam 1597.

Laughton 1890
> J.K. Laughton, 'Richard Hakluyt.' In: *Dictionary of national biograhy*. Vol. 24. London 1890, p. 11-12.

Laughton 1892
> J.K. Laughton, 'Anthony Jenkinson.' In: *Dictionary of national biography*. Vol. 29. London 1892, p. 307-309.

Lecouteux 1984
> Claude Lecouteux, 'Die Sage vom Magnetberg.' In: *Fabula* 25 (1984), p. 35-65.

Lengyel 1949
> E. Lengyel, *Siberië*. Transl. B. Raptschinsky. Den Haag 1949.

Linschoten 1914
> *Reizen van Jan Huyghen van Linschoten naar het noorden (1594-1595)*. Ed. S.P. L'Honoré Naber. 's-Gravenhage 1914.

Lucas 1937
> Henry S. Lucas, 'Mediaeval economic relations between Flanders and Greenland.' In: *Speculum* 12 (1937), p. 167-181.

Macrobius 1952
> Macrobius, *Commentary on the dream of Scipio*. Transl. William Harris Stahl. New York 1952.

Magnus 1555
> Olaus Magnus, *De gentibus septentrionalibus, earumque diversis statibus, conditionibus, moribus* [etc.]. Roma 1555.

Magnus 1558
> Olaus Magnus, *Historia de gentibus septentrionalibus. Sic in epitome redacta, ut non minus clarè quàm breviter quicquid apud septentrionales scitu dignum est, complectatur*. Antverpiae 1558.

Magnus 1562
> Olaus Magnus, *Historia de gentibus* [etc.]. Antverpiae 1562.

Magnus 1598(?)
> Olaus de Groote, *De wonderlijcke historie vande noordersche landen* [etc.]. Amsterdam (1598?)

Markham 1921
> Clements R. Markham, *The lands of silence. A history of arctic and antarctic exploration*. Cambridge 1921.

Marnef 1996
> Guido Marnef, *Antwerp in the age of reformation. Underground protestantism in a commercial metropolis 1550-1577*. Transl. J.C. Grayson. Baltimore and London 1996.

Martyr 1 1972
> Peter Martyr von Anghiera, *Acht Dekaden über die Neue Welt*. Transl. Hans Klingelhöfer. Vol. 1. Darmstadt 1972.

Massa-Gerritsz. 1924
[I. Massa] *Beschryvinghe vander Samoyeden landt in Tartarien* [etc.]. In: Hessel Gerritsz., *Beschryvinghe vander Samoyeden landt en Histoire du pays nommé Spitsberghe*. Ed. S.P. L'Honoré Naber. 's-Gravenhage 1924.

Maurer 1894
Konrad Maurer, 'Die Hölle auf Island.' In: *Zeitschrift des Vereins für Volkenkunde* 4 (1894), p. 256-269.

Mercator 1569 (1961)
Gerard Mercator, *Map of the world.* Duisburg 1569. Ed. B. van 't Hoff. Rotterdam, 's-Gravenhage 1961.

Mercator 1595 (1963)
Atlas sive cosmographicae meditationes de fabrica mundi et fabricati figura. 1595. Ed. A. de Smet. Brussel 1963.

Meskens 1994
Ad Meskens, *Wiskunde tussen renaissance en barok. Aspecten van wiskunde-beoefening te Antwerpen 1550-1620.* Antwerpen (1994).

Meurer 1991
Peter H. Meurer, *Fontes cartographici Orteliani. Das 'Theatrum Orbis Terrarum' von Abraham Ortelius und seine Kartenquellen.* Weinheim 1991.

Michov-Grynaeus 1532
Mathias a Michov, *De Sarmatica Asiana atque Europea libri duo.* In: Simon Grynaeus, *Novus orbis regionum et insularum veteribus incognitarum* [etc.]. Parisiis 1532.

Michow 1906
H. von Michow, 'Das erste Jahrhundert russischer Kartographie 1525-1631 und die Originalkarte des Anton Wied von 1542.' In: *Mitteilungen der geographischen Gesellschaft in Hamburg* 21 (1906), p. 1-61.

Michow 1907
H. Michow, 'Weitere Beiträge zur älteren Kartographie Russlands.' In: *Mitteilungen der geographischen Gesellschaft in Hamburg* 22 (1907), p. 125-172.

Montanus 1593
Benedictus Arias Montanus, *Antiquitatum Iudaicarum libri IX. In quîs, praeter Iudaeae, Hierosolymorum et Templi Salomonis accuratam delineationem, praecipui sacri ac profani gentis ritus describuntur.* 2nd ed. Lugdunum Batavorum 1593.

Morison 1978
Samuel Eliot Morison, *The great explorers. The European discovery of America.* New York 1978.

Moss 1981
Jean Dietz Moss, *Godded with God: Hendrik Niclaes and his Family of Love.* Philadelphia 1981.

Muller 1874
S. Muller Fz., *Geschiedenis der Noordsche Compagnie.* Utrecht 1874.

Münster 1550 (1968)
Sebastian Münster, *Cosmographei.* Bazel 1550. Ed. R. Oehme. Amsterdam 1968.

Nauwelaerts 1983
M.A. Nauwelaerts, 'Cornelius Scribonius.' In: *Moderne encyclopedie van de wereldliteratuur.* Vol. 8. Weesp, Antwerpen 1983, p. 318-319.

Nordenskiöld 1889 (1970)
N.A.E. Nordenskiöld, *Facsimile-atlas to the early history of cartography with reproductions of the most important maps printed in the 15 and 16 centuries.* Stockholm 1889. Fotomech. repr. Nendeln 1970.

Nouvelle biographie générale 22 1856, 35 1861
 Nouvelle biographie générale. Vols. 22 and 35. Paris 1858 and 1861.

Okhuizen 1992
 Edwin Okhuizen, 'Exploration and mapping of the northeast passage and northern Eurasia 15th-19th centuries.' In: Esko Häkli, Juha Nurminen and Nils-Erik Raurala (eds.), *The northeast passage. From the Vikings to Nordenskiöld*. Helsinki 1992, p. 10-49.

Olaus (de) Gro(o)te, Olaus Magnus
 see: Magnus

Oleson 1964
 Tryggvi J. Oleson, *Early voyages and northern approaches, 1000-1632*. London, New York 1964.

Ortelius 1570 (1964)
 Abraham Ortelius, *Theatrum orbis terrarum*. Antwerpen 1570. Ed. R.A. Skelton. Amsterdam 1964.

Ortelius 1571
 Abraham Ortelius, *Theatre, oft toonneel des aerdt-bodems*. (Antwerpen 1571).

Ortelius 1595
 Abrahamus Ortelius, *Additamentum quintum, theatri orbis terrarum*. Antverpiae 1595.

Ortelius 1887
 Abrahami Ortelii et virorum eruditorum ad eundem et ad Jacobum Colium Ortelianum epistulae [etc.] *(1524-1628)*. Ed. J.H. Hessels. Cantabrigia 1887.

Ortroy 1926
 F. van Ortroy, 'Les sources scientifiques de la cartographie mercatorienne.' In: *Mélanges d'histoire offerts à Henri Pirenne*. Vol. 2. Bruxelles 1926, p. 635-652.

Osley 1969
 A.S. Osley, Mercator. *A monograph on the lettering of maps* [etc.] *and a translation of Ghim's Vita Mercatoris*. London 1969.

Parker 1981
 Geoffrey Parker, *De Nederlandse opstand. Van beeldenstorm tot bestand*. 2nd ed. Utrecht, Antwerpen 1981.

Parry 1968
 J.H. Parry, *The European reconnaissance. Selected documents*. London, Melbourne 1968.

Paulus Diaconus 1878
 Paulus Diaconus, *Historia Langobardorum*. Hannover 1878.

Plantin 1 1883
 Ch. Plantin, *Correspondance*. Ed. M. Rooses and J. Denucé. Vol. 1. Antwerpen 1883.

Plinius 1 1967, 2 1969
 Pliny, *Natural history*. Transl. H. Rackham and D.E. Eichholz. Vols. 1 and 2. Cambridge, Mass. and London 1967, 1969.

Polo 1958
 The travels of Marco Polo. Transl. R. Latham. Harmondsworth 1958.

Postel 1560
 Guillaume Postel, *De la Republique des Turcs: et là ou l'occasion s'offrera, des meurs et loy de tous Muhamedistes*. Poitiers 1560.

Postel 1561
 Guilielmus Postellus, *Cosmographicae disciplinae compendium, in suum finem, hoc est ad Diuinae Prouidentiae certissimam demonstrationem conductus* [etc.]. Basileae 1561.

Postel 1969
 Guillaume Postel, *Le thresor des prophéties de l'univers*. Ed. F. Secret. La Haye 1969.

Postel 1985
 Guillaume Postel 1581-1981. Actes du colloque international d'Avranches 1981. Paris 1985.

Power 1968
  Eileen Power, 'The opening of the land routes to Cathay.' In: A.P. Newton (ed.), *Travel and travellers of the Middle Ages*. 4th ed. London 1968, p. 124-158.
Prims 8.1 1941, 8.2 1942
  F. Prims, *Geschiedenis van Antwerpen*. Vols. 8.1 and 8.2. Antwerpen 1941, 1942.
Ptolemaeus 1477 (1963)
  Claudius Ptolemaeus, *Cosmographia*. Bologna 1477. Ed. R.A. Skelton. Amsterdam 1963.
Ptolemaeus 1482 (1963)
  Claudius Ptolemaeus, *Cosmographia*. Ulm 1482. Ed. R.A. Skelton. Amsterdam 1963.
Ptolemaeus 1540 (1966)
  Ptolemaeus, *Cosmographia*. Ed. Seb. Münster. Bazel 1540. Ed. R.A. Skelton. Amsterdam 1966.
Purchas 11 1906, 12 1906, 13 1906
  Samuel Purchas, *Hakluytus posthumus or Purchas his pilgrimes. Contayning a history of the world in sea voyages and lande travells by Englishmen and others*. Vol. 11, 12 and 13. Glasgow 1906.
Ramusio 2 1574
  G.B. Ramusio, *Navigationi et viaggi*. Vol. 2. Venetia 1574.
Ramusio 1 1978, 4 1983
  G.B. Ramusio, *Navigazione e viaggi*. Ed. Marica Milanesi. Vols. 1 and 4. Torino 1978, 1983.
Rekers 1961
  Bernard Rekers, *Benito Arias Montano, 1527-1598. Studie over een groep spiritualistische humanisten in Spanje en de Nederlanden, op grond van hun briefwisseling*. Groningen 1961.
Resolutiën der Staten-Generaal 7 1923, 8 1925
  Resolutiën der Staten-Generaal van 1576 tot 1609. Ed. N. Japikse. Vols. 7 and 8. 's-Gravenhage 1923, 1925 (Rijks geschiedkundige publikatiën 55 and 57).
Roux 1984
  Jean-Paul Roux, *Histoire des Turcs. Deux mille ans du Pacifique à la Mediterranée*. Paris 1985.
Saxo 1 1979, 2 1980
  Saxo Grammaticus, *The history of the Danes*. Transl. Peter Fisher. Ed. Hilda Ellis Davidson. 2 vols. Cambridge 1979, 1980.
Schallenberg-van Huffel 1927
  W. Schallenberg-van Huffel, 'Balthasar de Moucheron.' In: P.C. Molhuysen a.o. (eds.), *Nieuw Nederlandsch biografisch woordenboek*. Vol. 7. Leiden 1927, col. 884-887.
Schilder 1984
  Günther Schilder, 'Development and achievements of Dutch northern and arctic cartography in the sixteenth and seventeenth centuries.' In: *Arctic* 37 (1984), 4, p. 493-514.
Schilder 1987
  Günter Schilder, *Monumenta cartographia Neerlandica*. Vol. 2. Alphen aan den Rijn 1987.
Secret 1973
  François Secret, 'Notes sur G. Postel.' In: *Bibiothèque d'humanisme et renaissance* 35 (1973), p. 85-101.
Secret 1981
  F. Secret, *Postelliana*. Nieuwkoop 1981.
Secret 1985
  F. Secret, 'Postel et l'origine des Turcs.' In: *Guillaume Postel 1581-1981. Actes du colloque international d'Avranches 1981*. Paris 1985, p. 301-306.
Semjonow n.d.
  Juri Semjonow, *De verovering van Siberië. Een epos van menschelijke hartstochten*. Transl. J.M. Palm. Den Haag n.d.

Seneca 2 1974
   The elder Seneca. Declamations. Transl. M. Winterbottom. Vol. 2. Cambridge, etc. 1974.
Sigurdsson 1984
   Haraldur Sigurdsson, 'Some landmarks in Icelandic cartography down to the end of the six-
   teenth century.' In: *Arctic* 37 (1984) 4, p. 389-401.
Skelton 1962
   R.A. Skelton, 'Mercator and English geography in the 16th century.' In: *Duisburger
   Forschungen* 6 (1962), p. 158-170.
Smedt 1 1950, 2 1954
   Oskar de Smedt, *De Engelse natie te Antwerpen in de 16e eeuw (1496-1592)*. 2 vols.
   Antwerpen 1950, 1954.
Smet 1962
   Antoine de Smet, 'Mercator à Louvain (1530-1552).' In: *Duisburger Forschungen* 6 (1962),
   p. 28-90.
Solinus 1572
   C. Iulius Solinus, *Polyhistor*. Ed. Martinus Ant. Delrius. Antverpiae 1572.
Starkov 1993
   V.F. Starkov, 'Early Russian-Dutch contacts in Arctic regions.' In: J. Braat, A.H. Huussen jr,
   a.o., *Russians and Dutchmen. Proceedings of the conference on the relations between Russia
   and the Netherlands. Rijksmuseum Amsterdam 1989*. Groningen 1993, p. 20-25.
State papers
   Calendar of state papers. Colonial series, East Indies, China and Japan, 1513-1616. Ed. W.
   Noël Sainsbury. London 1862.
Stoppelaar 1901
   J.H. de Stoppelaar, *Balthasar de Moucheron. Een bladzijde uit de Nederlandsche handels-
   geschiedenis tijdens den Tachtigjarigen Oorlog*. 's-Gravenhage 1901.
Taylor 1956
   E.G.R. Taylor, 'A letter dated 1577 from Mercator to Dee.' In: *Imago mundi* 13 (1956), p.
   56-68.
Taylor 1968
   E.G.R. Taylor, *Tudor geography 1485-1583*. New York 1968.
Thiele 1994
   Rudiger Thiele, 'Kosmographie als universale Wissenschaft. Zum Werk Gerhard Merca-
   tors.' In: Ruth Löffler, Gernot Tromnau a.o. (eds.), *Gerhard Mercator, Europa und die Welt.
   Ausstellung Duisburg 1994-1995*. Duisburg 1994, p. 15-36.
Thoroddsen 1 1897
   Th. Thoroddsen, *Geschichte der Isländischen Geographie*. Transl. August Gebhardt. Vol. 1:
   Die Isländische Geographie bis zum Schlusse des 16. Jahrhunderts. Leipzig 1897.
Thijs 1990
   A.K.L. Thijs, *Van geuzenstad tot katholiek bolwerk. Maatschappelijke betekenis van de
   kerk in contrareformatorisch Antwerpen*. Turnhout 1990.
Toorn-Piebenga 1987
   G.A. van der Toorn-Piebenga, 'Adam of Bremen. Account of a journey to the arctic region
   in the eleventh century.' In: *Circumpolar journal* 2 (1987), p. 18-30.
Tracy 1980
   James D. Tracy, *True ocean found. Paludanus's letters on Dutch voyages to the Kara Sea,
   1595-1596*. Minneapolis 1980.
Tromnau 1994
   Gernot Tromnau, 'Gerhard Mercator zum 400. Todestag.' In: Ruth Löffler, Gernot Trom-
   nau a.o. (eds.), *Gerhard Mercator, Europa und die Welt. Ausstellung Duisburg 1994-1995*.
   Duisburg 1994, p. 11-13.

Vaughan 1982
    Richard Vaughan, 'The Arctic in the Middle Ages.' In: *Journal of medieval history* 8 (1982),
    p. 313-342.
Veer 1 1917, 2 1917
    Gerrit de Veer, *Reizen van Willem Barents, Jacob van Heemskerck, Jan Cornelisz. Rijp en
    anderen naar het noorden (1594-1597)*. Ed. S.P. L'Honoré Naber. 2 vols. 's-Gravenhage
    1917.
Verduyn 1926
    W.D. Verduyn, *Emanuel van Meteren. Bijdrage tot de kennis van zijn leven, zijn tijd en het
    ontstaan van zijn geschiedwerk*. 's-Gravenhage 1926.
Verrycken 1990
    Amber Verrycken, *De middeleeuwse wereldverkenning*. Leuven, Amersfoort 1990.
Voet 1962
    Léon Voet, 'Les rélations commerciales entre Gérard Mercator et la maison Plantiniènne à
    Anvers.' In: *Duisburger Forschungen* 6 (1962), p. 171-232.
Voet 1 1969, 2 1972
    Léon Voet, *The golden compasses. A history and evaluation of the printing and publishing
    activities of the Officina Plantiniana at Antwerp*. 2 vols. Amsterdam 1969, 1972.
Wachsmuth 1967
    D. Wachsmuth, ΠΟΜΠΙΜΟΣ Ω ΔΑΙΜΩΝ. *Untersuchung zu den antiken Sakralhand-
    lungen bei Seereisen*. Berlin 1967.
Waghenaer 1592
    Lucas Jansz. Waghenaer, *Thresoor der zeevaert* [etc.]. Leyden 1592.
Waldseemüller 1903
    Martin Waldseemüller, *Die älteste Karte mit dem Namen Amerika aus dem Jahre 1507 und
    die Carta Marina aus dem Jahre 1516*. Ed. J. Fischer and F. v. Wieser. Innsbruck 1903.
Waldseemüller 1907 (1969)
    Martin Waldseemüller, *The cosmographiae introductio*. Ed. C.G. Herbermann. Introd. J.
    Fischer and F. von Wieser. New York 1907. Reprint 1969.
Wallis 1984
    Helen Wallis, 'England's search for the northern passages in the sixteenth and early seven-
    teenth centuries.' In: *Arctic* 37 (1984) 4, p. 453-472.
Wassenaer 1625
    Nicolaes à Wassenaer, *Historisch verhael aller gedencwaerdiger geschiedenissen* [etc.]. Vol. 8.
    Amsterdam 1625.
Wee 1 1963, 2 1963, 3 1963
    Herman van der Wee, *The growth of the Antwerp market and the European economy (four-
    teenth-sixteenth centuries)*. 3 vols. Den Haag 1963.
Wieder 1 1925
    F.C. Wieder (ed.), *Monumenta cartographica. Reproductions of unique and rare maps*. Vol. 1
    The Hague 1925.
Willan 1968
    T.S. Willan, *The early history of the Russian company, 1553-1603*. 2nd ed. Manchester 1968.
Williamson 1922
    J.A. Williamson, *A short history of British expansion*. London 1922.
Wijnroks 1993
    E.H. Wijnroks, 'Jan van de Walle and the Dutch silk-trade with Russia, 1578-1635.' In: J.
    Braat, A.H. Huussen jr, a.o., *Russians and Dutchmen. Proceedings of the conference on the
    relations between Russia and te Netherlands. Rijksmuseum Amsterdam 1989*. Groningen
    1993, p. 41-58.

Zeno-Major 1873

    The voyages of the Venetian brothers, Nicoló and Antonio Zeno, to the northern seas in the XlVth century, comprising the latest known accounts of the lost colony of Greenland; [etc.]. Transl. and ed. R.H. Major. London 1873.

Zieglerus-Krantzius 1583

    Jacobus Zieglerus, *Schondia, id est regionum et populorum septentrionalium* [etc.] *descriptio.* In: Albertus Krantzius, *Regnorum Aquilonanum* [etc.] *chronica.* Francofurti ad Moenum 1583.

Zweite 1980

    Arnim Zweite, *Marten de Vos als Maler. Ein Beitrag zur Geschichte der Antwerpener Malerei in der zweiten Hälfte des 16. Jahrhunderts.* Berlin 1980.

Illustrations